# L.O.S.S.
## *Life's Opportunity to Soul Search*

by Misty Nichols

Chalk Creek Press
Nashville, TN
2016

Published by Chalk Creek Press
Nashville, TN

CHALK
CREEK
PRESS

First Edition
April 2016

Edited by Susannah Felts and Jennifer Chesak
Cover design by Kevin Robinson Creative
Illustrations by Kevin Robinson Creative

www.MistyNichols.com
www.facebook.com/lifesopportunitytosoulsearch
www.instagram.com/misty_nichols

ISBN 978-0-9972074-0-8

To Kris.
My brother, my friend, my inspiration.

*The burden of suffering seems a tombstone hung about our necks, while in reality it is only the weight which is necessary to keep down the diver while he is hunting for pearls.*

—JEAN PAUL RICHTER

# Contents

# Introduction

You've experienced a loss, it hurts beyond measure and you don't know how you can possibly go on. I know. I've been there too. I wish I could take away all of your pain and make you feel better instantly, but there's no way to make that happen. This will be a journey, and you are at the starting point now. There is no easy way out of the pain. In fact, you don't want to find your way out. Finding your way out of the pain would mean you are ignoring or blocking necessary emotions, realizations, and opportunities for growth. This will only lead to unnecessary, prolonged suffering. Suffering is not progressive healing. Suffering is like putting a plug on the flow of knowledge, growth, and understanding that is naturally available to you at all times, especially in times of hardship. I'm not saying you won't suffer for a while, or maybe a long while. Suffering is inevitable, but I don't believe that suffering should last forever. If you ignore the pain and grieving process now, it will creep back into your life later. Now is the time to find your way *through* the pain. Not in a forceful way, but with a nurturing awareness through your experience. No doubt it's going to be a painful and difficult ride, with a lot of confusing moments spent with uncertain thoughts and seemingly uncontrollable emotions. Even though they may be hard to understand in the midst of our most difficult moments, our emotions have a way of protecting and healing us. Each emotion you experience is important from here on, and there is so much wisdom to gain through the coming days.

My intention is that this book will help bring some clarity to your journey and will give you the tools to cope, heal, and live your best and healthiest life. This book is for anyone who has experienced a loss and wants to grieve in a healthy way, make the best of the situation, be better because of it, grow from the experience, and find the lessons within it all. I'm not only speaking of a loss associated with a death. A loss can also mean a divorce, a loss of a career, a relationship, or a loss of self or identity. The reason I can give you this information is because I also have felt the pain of loss. I have experienced real pain from life experiences, some of them very much out of my control. I have asked every question under the sun. I questioned the existence of a higher power, what my purpose was, and what my identity was. In my darkest moments, I questioned whether my life was worth living. I have also hurt beyond measure and wondered if there was any way I could possibly climb the rugged mountain of grief that suddenly stood before me.

I'm here to say that I made it through the pain and up the mountain. I accepted my losses and found peace within it all. I conquered my fears and found myself. I found the purpose for my life and am proud of where I am today. It is my hope that the following pages will encourage you to do the same, all while progressing toward a deeper understanding. This will, in turn, help you regain your life. A life maybe even *better* than you had before your loss. Yes, it is absolutely possible.

From my experience, L.O.S.S. = **L**ife's **O**pportunity to **S**oul **S**earch.

I experienced multiple losses within twelve months, so I had a crash course on how to surrender, search, fight, survive, and evolve into a new and better person.

At times it seemed the only option I had was to sink to the depths of depression and let the pain consume me. Sometimes it felt like I was getting nowhere, and there was no place to even strive to go. Grief can have a way of making us feel that way. But fortunately, I found ways to trudge up my life mountain to a better vantage point. It's not easy. There is no short path. No downhill climb to the top.

I documented my life during my darkest days of my brother's suicide, my divorce, and my father's stroke, which left him incapable of speaking. All of these events happened within a year's time. Through these events, I lost a best friend, trust in others, a career I was planning on, the life I had once known, and the future I had envisioned. Also through these trials, I documented my happiest days by way of large or small milestones and any positive changes that were developing in my life. Sometimes the smallest things I would do in a day would help me cope and keep me moving forward. Some things just clicked and truly made a difference. I wrote these things down and journaled as much as I could about my emotions, struggles, heartaches, and victories.

I realized that the losses and adversities I had experienced were the catalysts to my growth as a person. I had the choice to grow or stay in a state of empty suffering. I chose the route of growth, and a shift occurred within. I became who I really was supposed to be. I saw my life from a deeper and clearer perspective. Life made more sense. Life was more than a bunch of mundane days with routine moments. I expanded as a person, and I finally found and connected with what I now define and experience as God. I found faith and strength in the process of my life. I found forgiveness and gratitude, which turned out to be the most important feelings I could express and experience. This book started out as my journal entries. Writing about my journey was my way of processing and understanding my grief. It was my way of introspectively piecing my life back together. All the while I was finding me. The me I wanted to be.

Since everyone's life losses are different, everyone's grieving and healing processes are different, so in turn, everyone's life lessons and perspectives are different too. But I've come to learn that human losses have common themes with similar processes and key points, and we can learn from each other's struggles. Everyone who suffers a loss has an opportunity for tremendous growth. A loss can push the limits of our potential and unlock the doors in our minds and hearts that were maybe at one time closed and unexplored. External interference and our own emotions can cloud us, but blessings abound when we stop and listen to our knowledge. Our deepest pain can become our deepest understanding. I'm not saying that we are prescribed a loss in order to receive an opportunity, especially in the case of losing a loved one, as there truly is no justification for that loss. Nobody should lose a son, daughter, or a brother or sister too soon. But we are given a choice as to how we handle our losses. The losses we suffer offer us an opportunity to expand and learn from the experience, as opposed to eternal suffering. I want others to know that they are not alone. I want others to not give up on the beauty of their journey. I want others to know that LOSS really is life's opportunity to soul search.

Take comfort in knowing others have walked a similar path as you. We can learn from each other, and that is the beauty in the sharing of our stories. Experiencing a major loss can set you back to square one. It's like seeking answers in a new and foreign world. A loss may present the option to sink or swim, or in my mountain analogy, which I will explain later, "climb or die." I want everyone to choose to climb.

The first half of this book is my personal story of my losses. Then the second half of the book describes "24 Truths," which were the things that helped me survive, grow, and reach a new perspective. They helped me gain a new life. My story and my pain will forever be a part of me, just as yours will be a part of you.

# CHAPTER ONE

# My brother

*January 19th, 2012. The day my world stopped turning.*

My husband and I had just returned from a vacation to St. John, in the U.S. Virgin Islands. We had been there once before in 2007 and we'd fallen in love with the island. Back in Nashville, we dove back into our busy, stressful lives of running a custom event lighting company, where we designed and set up creative lighting for weddings and other high-end events around town. After wearing every hat in the business, I had recently taken over as the office manager and bookkeeper.

A few months prior, we had been approached by another event rental company in town about their interest in buying our business. We were very much considering this opportunity, as the business had become very stressful for us. So we met with an attorney that afternoon to discuss the legalities of selling it. While we were waiting in the attorney's lobby, tears welled up in my eyes when I briefly mentioned to my husband how my brother was doing. Kris had been battling depression and alcohol addiction for the last 12 years. He was 29 years old and he was currently in the midst of a streak of bad days. When I was on the island, my family had been updating me that he was at a low point, and that he'd been drinking and was very depressed. A few days before, I had even texted my brother, asking him to come stay with my husband and me for a while in Nashville. He gracefully declined. He never wanted to be a "burden" to us. He always told me "Misty, everything's going to be okay." I always tried to believe him. No matter how bad Kris hurt, he always loved his family. The last thing he wanted to do was to hurt or worry any of us. I admired him immensely for his unwavering integrity and compassion for people. He was a fair man. He loved me, and he wasn't afraid to tell me so. We were a tight-knit family, and over the years Kris's addictions and behavior seemed to consume and dictate our every thought and action.

We wanted desperately for him to be happy and live up to his potential. I lived nine hours away from Kris but still tried to "save" him in any way I could. My parents would leave their small town in Kansas and drive down to Arkansas time and time again, in hopes of pulling him out of his dangerous, depressive, self-abusive funk. They would beg him to stop drinking, stop hurting himself, to just stop. Relentless love—a never ending well of forgiveness and heartache, all in one. If Kris was having a good day, we all had a good day. If Kris was having a bad day, the four of us had a bad day. He did have his periods of sobriety, but for whatever reason, a relapse unfortunately always happened at some point. On his bad days, we could all feel his pain from miles away.

When we couldn't get in touch with him, we would worry. *Is he in trouble? Is he hurt? Is he dead?* The four of us would debate how to handle the situation. Whether or not to drive to Arkansas to help him. Whether or not to let him go. Should we press him to go to another rehab? Does he need religion? Do we use tough love? Do we get angry? Or do we hold back? Do we encourage him to find different friends? Or do we just be his friend? We walked a fine line, trying to help and give advice, yet not wanting to push him away. Kris always respected us as best he could. He would listen. He wouldn't fight. Yet he was going to do things his way. He knew no other way. He believed another rehab wouldn't help him, and I honestly question if it would have either.

Kris had an ability to think beyond any shallowness of mankind. His depth took him to the far corners of his mind, and I enjoyed our philosophical conversations. Kris was an adventurer and an explorer, both mentally and physically. He was the one who would fearlessly climb the secluded, untouched land of the mountainside. Not for the selfish glory in it, but for the invaluable experience of freedom. He innately understood nature's healing ability. He embraced the kindred connection he had while in the wide-open spaces of this world, whether in a Kansas wheat field or a Colorado mountainside. This is where he connected with God, himself, and the deepest part of his soul. All was well in these moments. The trivial rat race of society did not exist in those times of solitude in the outdoors. He had a connection with God, one I believe I understood. Kris stayed true to himself, but

3

he had a vice. A vice that he could never quite understand enough to let go.

The good times with Kris were many. I was closest with him growing up as a child. We would play after school in our back yard, digging in the dirt, hanging out in our tree house, riding our three wheeler, catching tadpoles, walking our miniature ponies around our small town, or trying to create an adventure, such as attempting to run away from home on our scooter with one partially flat tire. We made it two blocks down the road and decided we were hungry and it wasn't a good idea. We turned back home. We had no reason to run away. We simply wanted an adventure. A story to tell. Those were innocent days. He was the sweetest little brother. We had an incredible bond. We invented things together, we explored together, we put on magic shows for my parents. I remember my parents had just bought a new appliance and still had the large rectangular box in the garage. I decided it was a perfect prop for a magic trick performance. Kris was going to play a disappearing and reappearing act. I set the box up outside against the house, and we practiced our trick. I asked Kris to get in the box and stay standing so Mom and Dad could see him. Then once I closed the box, he was to hunch down to the bottom as low as he could go. (He was five years old.) Then, I had a pre-cut slit in the center of the box that I would dramatically ram a shovel blade through and pull back out. Then, Kris would stand up, and I would open up the box. Ta-da! Kris would step out of the box unscathed! We executed our performance without a hitch. My parents smiled and applauded. It was pure magic.

Kris wasn't always my puppet. He also got me to do things with him that fed his boy personality. He taught me how to make slingshots and fight the Indians in our front yard. I'd hide in couch forts with him and shoot fake BB guns at the bad guys. We would dig in our back yard for "ancient artifacts," which translated to digging up rocks. We were fine with that. We would set up the tent in the basement and pretend to be camping in the woods. We played swords in the living room, and I swung a little hard one time and knocked his sword (stick) out of his hand; it went flying into my mom's antique lamp shade and shattered it. We both got in trouble when our parents got home, yet we still giggled under our breaths as we got our spankings. We loved each other as children. We had each other's backs. And we continued to love each other as adults.

As we got older, Kris and I remained friends, but problems developed in his life that I could not relate to. He hid his problems from us for many years. From the age of 13, he suffered from depression. Though he did not tell us about that pain, he did write about it extensively. He began masking his mental turmoil with alcohol and drugs. He had found an outlet. A way to feel "okay" for a little while. A way to dissolve the anxiety, the insecurities, the helplessness, and the feelings of inferiority. A way to survive in the midst of the gray cloud of depression. He lived on a dangerous, slippery slope, with a foot in two worlds, never sure where or how to ground his feet and root his soul. His was a disassembled heart that never found a way to accept love for himself.

For years I had an analogy in my head to describe my family. I pictured the five of us as birds in a small birdcage, incessantly flying around, trying to make sense of our lives. As we made attempts at freedom, we would only find ourselves following patterns. Patterns of trying to help him. We would try over and over; we would get our hopes up, just to get let down. With our wings flapping against the wire entrapment, we failed time and time again. None of us could find the door to let ourselves out, let Kris out, or to be free from the cyclical bondage. Free from the pain. We soon became almost numb to the discontented nature of our lives. I did not have the answer. It got to the point where there seemed to not be an answer at all. I couldn't let go though. I couldn't reject my family, no matter how painful and emotionally taxing the situation. Love can be tough. Family love can be tougher. It seemed impossible to walk away, to not care so much, to not love so much, to not try till our dying breath to "fix" the problem. Addiction and depression can be a slow, painful disease that all family members watch with no answers, no timeline, no safety net, and seemingly no open door to the birdcage.

After my husband and I had our appointment with our attorney, I went back to the office to catch up on all the work and emails that had piled up over the course of our vacation. In the meantime, my parents and sister were once again driving down to Arkansas from Kansas. We were concerned. Kris had been on a drinking binge for days. He had become more difficult to communicate with. He was losing hope.

My sister updated me with text messages as they got closer to Kris's small country farmhouse. We knew it was serious by the conversations they were having with him. We knew we were on the brink of something bad happening, but we didn't know what.

"Get him out of there, something bad is going to happen!" I wrote.

When they were in his drive, she wrote back: "Misty, it's all dark."

Shortly after, around 6 p.m. she called me. I don't remember her words, but it was over. My family was 20 minutes too late. My brother had shot himself in his living room recliner.

This was the same recliner he would sit in each evening and read self-help books such as *Power of Your Subconscious Mind*, books by Napoleon Hill and positive quotes by Henry David Thoreau, his AA book, and the Bible, which he read from front to back. Just a year earlier I had spent a week with him in January at his house. I sat on the couch, he sat in that recliner. We had a fire blazing in the wood-burning stove he had installed a few years earlier. His fat cat, Otis, lay in the middle of the floor. He talked about his problems, his concerns, his life. I talked about mine. We listened to each other. We read. We wrote down goals. We bonded. He wanted to find love. He wanted stability. He wanted to learn to love himself. He just wanted to feel better. So he ended his pain on January 19th.

I threw my cell phone to the floor and ran through the front doors of our office and out into the cold. I ran. I ran hard. I couldn't stop. I ran along the ditch by the railroad tracks in the dark. I couldn't even cry at this point. Adrenaline shot through my entire body and mind. I couldn't breathe, and I couldn't think rationally. All I could do was run, as if I could run away from this incomprehensible reality that I suddenly faced. Then I collapsed in the dark ditch. I pounded my fist on the ground, screaming. One of the men working on the railroad heard me, so he pulled up and asked if I was all right. I could barely talk. "Family emergency," I said. "I'm okay." He drove off into the night. I definitely was not okay. I suppose I knew he couldn't do anything to help at that point. I was alone. "Where are you? Kris, where are you?" I shouted. "I need to know!" My panicked mind began working in extreme, helpless ways.

After some time spent pacing and lying in that ditch, I called my husband. I knew he had gone to see a songwriter's show with a friend. Luckily he answered and came to get me immediately. He was panicked and scared. He did his best, but had no idea how to cope with me or his own emotions at that time. He finally got me in the car and took me home. He got our suitcase down from the attic, and I threw some mismatched clothes in it. I was incapable of packing, planning, or understanding what was in store. All I knew was I needed to get to Arkansas. I couldn't think straight. I shook my head and said, "No, no, no, no." It now hurt too bad to accept it. Denial was certainly the only way I could survive the shock that my brother was lying in his home with blood pouring out of his head— lifeless, nine hours away from me, and I *wasn't there* to hold his warm hand one last time. I didn't have a chance to say my final goodbye, to tell him how much I loved him. My parents and sister had that opportunity, but I missed out. The guilt set in. I had just spent ten days soaking up the sun on a beautiful island while my brother was suffering beyond my comprehension, contemplating whether or not his life was worth living another day. Apparently, in his eyes, it wasn't. We loaded up the truck and left for Arkansas around 8:30 p.m.

We made it halfway to my aunt and uncle's place, where my parents and sister were staying. Kris lived just 15 minutes from there. My husband and I were too tired to drive any longer, so we stayed somewhere between Memphis and Little Rock in a little motel off the side of the interstate. Hands down, worst night of my life. I sat on the side of the bathtub rocking back and forth, shaking. Finally, I made my way to bed. Out of sheer exhaustion, I was able to sleep maybe an hour.

The next morning was a blur as we continued to head west. I hung my head most of the way and sobbed. We finally got to my uncle's long, dirt, country drive. I remember the sound of our truck tires against the gravel as we slowly approached the house. My heart was pounding. I was terrified of what I would see, what I would hear, and how I would feel. I was terrified to see my family members' faces. My mom and sister met us in the drive. My knees buckled when I stepped out of the truck. I couldn't even hold my own weight up. My mother's sorrowful face. My sister's eyes full of grieving tears. The dreaded day had arrived. So much sadness. Impossible to comprehend all at once. My sadness was enough, but to witness my mother's pain was unbearable.

She held my shoulders. "Misty, we lost him."

I nodded. We lost the battle. The three of us held each other.

I went inside to find my dad. He was sitting alone in a rocking chair in the sunroom, staring at the crackling embers in the wood-burning stove. The room was warm and quiet. Dad looked strangely calm—like the calm after a severe storm. Although he sat in a relaxed position, I sensed he was lost. I understood that feeling. He didn't seem afraid, just simply forlorn. Nothing had sunk in yet. He hadn't slept a wink since they'd found my brother, so he was extremely exhausted. My poor dad. My heart ached for him. He tried relentlessly for years to save his only son. His best friend. The one he connected with most. He would have given his life. I held my dad. He held me. We then cried together.

"My baby girl, my baby girl," he said.

I felt his pain along with mine. We both felt Kris's pain. I've never held my dad so tight.

I walked out of the house and my first instinct was to hike about a quarter of a mile down the road to the creek, where Kris used to live in a little cabin a few years back. I had visited him a few times while he lived there; he loved it. He loved the creek and the Indian history that the land held. He collected old arrowheads along the bank and would swim and fish in the cold, crystal water. For about ten feet above the water's edge, it's all rocks. Some of them have fossilized and contain pieces of plant or animal life material. All sizes, all shapes, all colors. All I wanted to do was lie on those rocks by the water. So I did. I lay facedown and listened to the creek. The rocks were cold against my face and body, but I didn't want to leave. I held a rock in my hand and grazed my fingers against its smooth surface. Tears rolled down my cheeks. The rock fit my hand perfectly, as if it was meant for me to hold. It had within it a pattern of long thin lines, like the wing of a bird. Something had died and had been preserved within this rock. I put it in my pocket.

*This* is where Kris now lived. Not by that creek specifically, but in nature, in my mind, in spirit. He was still close to me. I knew then that I could find him by the water, in the trees, and in the starlit sky. I could find him wherever I wanted to. This was my first moment with him in spirit form. His mark will also remain. No, I would never again see him alive on this earth, but I could forever have a connection with him if I chose to. It would be different, it would take time, but it was up to me to feel it. For a brief moment by that creek, I felt secure and grounded. It was all I could ask for.

We stayed at my uncle's house that night. I lay in bed and longed for my brother. I wanted one more chance to save him. I thought of things I should have said, shouldn't have said, and things I wished I could ask him. I wanted to ask him what it was like to die. I wanted to ask him if there was a heaven. What does it feel like? Can you hear me? Do you know my pain? Do you have regrets? But all I could hear were my aunt's wind chimes on the front porch dancing softly with the breeze. It was a peaceful sound. Like a lullaby. I finally drifted off to sleep for a few hours.

We drove to Kansas that next morning. But before we left, we grabbed an outfit from Kris's house for him to wear for his service. Although I knew he would have wanted to wear a T-shirt, blue jeans and boots, we dressed him in a long-sleeved gray shirt and black pants that he'd worn to my wedding five years before. I thought back to how handsome he'd looked that day as he walked my mom down the aisle. I held on to that shirt most of the way to Kansas. It still smelled of his cologne. It was soft. It was him. I held him close.

Shortly after arriving to my parents' house, we planned for the funeral. We had to make quick decisions. I was living in a timeless moment while the rest of the world un-remorsefully sped by. At the funeral, I read my brother's personal mission statement, which he'd written just one year prior while we were walking through the woods in Arkansas:

> *My mission is to live a life of adventure, courage, integrity, faith and love. I will treat myself and others with respect. I will always search for God's will, and fearlessly follow it. I will always do the best I can with what I have at hand. I will have gratitude for what I have and faith that more good things will come.*

—Kris Nichols, 1.27.11

I debated whether or not to read his mission statement for a couple of reasons. One reason being that it was personal to him. He didn't write it for the world to see. He did have it taped up on his living room wall to pass by every day and read, but his intention wasn't for a lot of people to read it. He kept it on his wall as a reminder to himself of the man he wanted to be. To hold himself accountable. But I wanted people to know him. Know his heart like I did. Know his intentions as a man and realize that, although someone may have some turmoil in his life such as an addiction, a mental disease, a vice, it doesn't mean he isn't a good person. It doesn't mean he doesn't try or sincerely want things to be better.

I also hesitated to exploit Kris's words due to the potential judgment and criticism of others. There is a massive misconception, or a stigma, on those who struggle with mental illness, depression, and addiction. I've seen firsthand how difficult it is for someone to overcome, cope, and survive through these illnesses. Nobody truly wants to die—unless maybe he or she suffers from a mental disease, an illness that affects his or her emotional well-being. Some may think that depression is simply a state of mind that can be fixed by way of thought. Although I am a huge advocate of positive thinking and believe it has a profound impact on our mental health, I do believe there's a deeper and more complex reason and solution for chronic depression. Depression is not a character flaw. It is not caused by bad parenting. It often times is not a choice. For some there is no easy fix. There may be biochemical and genetic links to the disease that cause imbalances in the brain's neurotransmitters. This could, simply put, cause an unfortunate disconnect between people, places, and feelings. Hopelessness and worthlessness creeps in.

Kris had every opportunity in the world—a loving family, friends who cared about him, a steady job, a strong body, and a sharp mind. There was a deep reason for his pain. I hope in my heart that one day we are more able to help those whom suffer from this feeling of disconnect, and I hope the stigma and judgment dissolves. I hope that people will not be ashamed to admit their pain and seek help, just as we do with any other ailment or disease. Nobody should suffer. And nobody should want to die. I chose to read

Kris's mission statement as a way of honoring who he truly was beneath the layers of pain and mental anguish—his earthly problems.

As the sun shone down on us that January day, we watched the casket slowly lower into the ground, and we sang "I'll Fly Away." I pictured him gazing down on us smiling and saying, *Yes, I've flown away to a better place. I'm free from the cage. Everything is going to be okay.*

Yes, Kris was free from that birdcage that we as a family occupied and tried to survive in for years. But was I free from the cage? I felt like my family was still in that cage, but now there were only four of us. I didn't know how to escape from that bondage of pain. From that frenzy of emotion. The cage. Or was that cage door open, and we just weren't sure how to spread our wings and fly out just yet?

The following days, we continued to face the emotional challenges and necessary business that came with losing a loved one. A few days after the funeral, we drove back down to Arkansas to clean out Kris's house and garage. We pulled up to his little yellow two-story farmhouse. It sat on a stretch of land off a dirt road a few miles north of a small town. He loved that house. It was peaceful there. Nothing to interfere with the freedom of the breeze, the bowl of stars, or the view of the sunrise and sunset. I stood in his front yard and retraced a memory of watching one of those sunsets with him a year before. It was January. I remembered his voice. He'd commented on how bright the stars were in the country and the beauty of the fading orange sun falling behind the western sky. I sure was going to miss that voice.

I slowly walked into my brother's house, knowing he would not be there to greet me at the door with his smile. His scent still lingered in the air and visions rushed through my mind as I thought about his final hours in that house. The most recent book he was reading lay on the coffee table, open and face down on the last pages he'd read. The book was *The Road Less Traveled & Beyond* by M. Scott Peck. What were his last thoughts? How quickly things can change in an instant. With one decision. A decision of yes or no. A pull of the trigger. I stared at his recliner. I then pictured my parents and sister finding him lifeless. What must have that been like? It's as if I were there. The screams, the panic, the adrenaline, the nightmare. His cat, Otis, was the only witness to the gunshot. And he will never tell. My parents said Kris looked content and peaceful when they found him sitting in that chair. His palms folded restfully in his lap. He was finally free.

In his office, I found orange, green and yellow sticky notes lining the perimeter of his desk and bookshelf like sacred ornaments on a tree. Each had meaningful hand-written quotes by Henry David Thoreau, Johnny Cash, Jesus, himself, and others. His bookshelf was a shrine of energy, full of information and wisdom. It was alive. I wanted to be in it. I wanted to search and be filled with knowledge. I wanted to live in Kris's world for a while.

His clipboard was lying on his desk with current invoices to send out to his customers and receipts from recent purchases. Every item in that house took on a new feeling and a new sense of meaning for me. These things were his. They were here when he was alive, and they remained when he was dead. He was the last one to touch them. I tried to be as respectful as possible while going through his personal items. We boxed up his belongings and hesitatingly threw some things into trash bags, which we labeled "burn." Just as he had asked us to do.

My mom, sister, and I went through his clothing. Although Kris didn't put much value into any material things, especially clothing, those items meant something to us. Going through his closet and dresser drawers was a sentimental journey. His jeans, his boots, his T-shirts—the ones with rips, holes, and stains—they were proof of his life, proof of his hard work and strength. His boots had walked many miles and held many stories of tragedy and triumph. We had bought some of the shirts and shoes as Christmas gifts. We couldn't decide what to keep or get rid of, so we shoved all of his clothes into big black trash bags, and threw them in the truck bed to take back home. We would sort through them at a later date. A much, much later date.

After cleaning out his house, we headed to his workshop about 30 yards from his house. Here we discussed his tools, trucks, trailers, and motorcycle. I knew he would want us to just give it all away or throw it out. Some of it we did. For the few things he did care about, he'd written in his last testament as to whom the items should go. Kris's belongings suddenly became more than just things to us. They became the last remaining tangible items of him. We needed some things to hold onto physically. Things we could touch, smell, and feel. Even an old book, a pair of shoes, or a hammer. We wanted to hold it all, at least for a little while.

Once everything was cleaned out, we headed back to Kansas for the very last time. We formed a melancholy parade: my parents' vehicle, Kris's trucks, trailer, and a rented box truck. Everything that was his was now in our hands. I looked behind me and said goodbye to his Arkansas home, which I assumed I would never see again. We had six hours to sit with our thoughts, asking ourselves, *What's next?* I knew January 19th would always bear a scar. My heart will always bear a deep, significant scar.

After a couple of weeks with my family, I headed back down to Nashville to resume my life. Having no idea what was in store, I lived in mental and emotional turmoil for the next few months. I'd have an okay day followed by a bad day. A constant state of ups and downs. I buried myself in my work, staying at the office late into the night. It was a distraction, a way for my mind to stay focused on something that felt like progress. I was physically alive, but emotionally and spiritually I was dead. I walked through the mall and grocery store as if I had the words "my brother just killed himself" on my forehead. I imagined people could see through me and knew my story, yet did nothing to help. I was broken and unfixable. It was like one of those dreams where you are walking around naked in public. I was vulnerable and exposed, and I hated it.

*To live in hearts we leave behind is not to die.*

—THOMAS CAMPBELL

# CHAPTER TWO

# My husband

In order to cope with my brother's passing and the extreme guilt, confusion, and grief that followed, I searched for answers in books whenever I had the chance. I wanted to learn. I wanted to understand. I wanted to grow through the pain. I put positive notes on my computer at work, on my bathroom mirror, and in my car. This did help me, but there was a big piece missing. Part of that missing piece was a connection with my husband.

His problem-solver personality couldn't fix this issue of my brother being gone. He also couldn't fix my grief. It got to the point where I didn't care any more, and he certainly didn't either. Sure, I wanted it to be different, but it wasn't. I needed him. I needed a supportive partner, but he wasn't able to be that person for me. I didn't know how to fix the disconnection between us and the lack of love that I experienced. I was selfishly trying to take care of me, and he was selfishly taking care of him. He didn't seem to find it necessary to listen to me, to hold me, or to ask me how I was doing. I no longer existed in his mind. I felt like a lost cause, and more or less a burden on his existence.

I missed my brother. I was trying to comprehend the notion of "forever." I also missed having a husband who I connected with. I do not wallow in self-pity. I consider myself a strong and independent individual. This was not a scenario of me feeling sorry for myself or needing someone else to fix me or live in misery with me, but I needed a little support and love from the one who'd vowed to be by my side "through thick and thin." He failed. I failed too. We worked against each other.

I should have taken more initiative to find the answers for us. But I felt he had emotionally shut me out. He was ready to move on. It had only been two months. I was still trying to make sense of the loss. He wasn't tied to Kris like I was. I resented him and was angry at him for his lack of compassion and failure to understand. It was a complicated matter of heartache and turmoil for both of us.

I tried meeting with counselors but gave up after a couple of sessions. I wanted more obvious progress. I wanted answers, something to take home with me to work on, to help grow through the experience towards happiness. Something was very wrong in my marriage, and we couldn't fix it. It had been a bit rocky for years. We'd had good days and bad days and hung onto the idea of love—to the *idea* that maybe it would get better and love and happiness would eventually find us. Our lives were forcing us into a change, and each of us were taking a separate path. But both of us had parents who stuck through the tough times and were married for life, so a divorce just didn't seem possible.

We struggled to meet in the middle, compromise, and understand each other. All in all, we failed to love deeply. Two people had grown apart and tried to find themselves in the murk of anger, loss, and sadness. I suppose my deep concern for Kris and my undying efforts to try to save him got in the way of my marriage at times. I didn't know what else to do. At the time I didn't know I was slowly losing my husband as well. Suddenly it was too late. As my needs were not met, I became contemptuous towards him, a dangerous place to be. I couldn't understand why he couldn't just listen, look me in the eye, and care a little, hold my hand, ask me how I'm feeling. He was no longer available as a husband, partner, or friend. Eventually, we lived in a house full of hate. I wanted out, but didn't know how. I was afraid. Incredibly afraid.

Luckily, through all of this turmoil, I did have one thing—instinct, and a tiny glimmer of hope. I knew deep down there were answers, and I knew I could find my way to a better life. I didn't want to be a victim of circumstance, an unhealthy woman who couldn't overcome the challenges laid out in front of her. I have never been one to give up, but my marriage was one problem I couldn't solve. It was impossible for me to find the answers I needed while living in an unhealthy environment with my husband. It was impossible for him to find the answers he needed too. My marriage was suffocating me emotionally, draining the energy I needed to help myself, to heal myself. I wrote in my journal almost every day. I wrote down my internal experiences as I moved along. I expressed my sadness. My confusion. I wrote down the dreams I had that felt symbolic. My books and my journals became a very important part of me. I took them everywhere. They were my life support, my friends. I had to express myself somehow, and writing became an outlet. I'd oftentimes find a solution and some kind of hope by the end of a journal entry. Other times I just needed a safe place to land my sorrows.

Four months after Kris passed, I was separated from my husband. It was mid-May, and I walked out of the office for the very last time. We'd had a long, stressful phone conversation, and there was nothing left to say to attempt to mend all that was broken. I wanted to die that day. I had lost all hope.

I said, "Kris, I understand. I now know what it feels like to not want to live. I have nothing to live for. I do not blame you. I want to be where you are now." I came to terms with his death in that moment. I now had a personal experience on which to base my compassion for him. A feeling of complete desperation. A place where all is gray and the future is incomprehensible. In this moment of understanding, I was also relieved. This was the closest I came to possibly feeling how Kris had felt on a somewhat regular basis.

I had already planned on going home around that time to help my father cut the wheat he and Kris had planted. Kris had planned to move back to Kansas at some point, so when it came time to cut, my sister and I went home to help bring in the harvest in honor of him. It was also my opportunity to get away for a while to try to sort my life out. I needed to get away from a man I barely knew anymore. He looked the same, but his presence was cold, angry, and sad. So I drove 13 hours to western Kansas. I had a long time to think, to fear, and to question life, death, and my future. There were no answers. But in some weird way, driving away was freedom. Once I started out on the road, I wanted to drive till I reached the edge of the earth, to somehow be met with a new life. But I needed to be home with my family. I had a destination: home. That was one thing—the only thing—I knew at that time. Follow this road, in this definite direction, and I would be in the place where I needed to be. After that, who knew? At that point, anything was possible.

A few hours down the road, I took the exit for Hopkinsville, Kentucky. I had wanted to see Edgar Cayce's gravesite for years, and I figured now was the time. I had nobody to tell me "no," or "we don't have time," or ask me "why." So I drove 45 minutes out of the way to get to his burial site. I had read Cayce's biography, *There Is a River*, a few years before, and was fascinated by his life and dedication to helping others through his unique gifts. I wondered where he'd been laid to rest—this famous man with such amazing and controversial talents, who grew up on this Kentucky land I now stood on. It took me a while to find his grave. I was in search of a tall marker, an obvious burial site that would forever be a testament to his meaningful life so that others such as I could honor his life and works. I quickly realized I had been mistaken. His tombstone was small. It was average. It looked insignificantly boring, like all the others that lined the cemetery. His wife lay beside him, with a stone that looked like his. I was both disappointed and relieved. I thought of my husband and the priorities in our marriage. I often felt pressure to be something better than I was—something more significant and more successful. Of course this can be a good thing, but I never found contentment or security in the direction I was heading. I never felt I was good enough. I felt pressure to "be somebody." I exhaled and smiled. *So this is where we go,* I thought. Regardless of status, fame, or money, this is where we go. In the ground. And the afterlife remains a mystery. I thought, *I am somebody.* Nobody else on earth can judge me. I am the one who judges whether or not I am a success, whether I am happy or fulfilled. I thought that if there was a God who would judge me when I die, he would understand. And more importantly, he would not judge me by my notoriety or my societal or monetary successes. He would know my troubles and my honest attempts to be a good person. What mattered was in my heart. I have a good heart, and I think God knows that.

I said my goodbyes to Edgar and his wife. As I walked back to my car, the Italian proverb, "At the end of the game, the king and the pawn go back into the same box," kept trailing through my head. Edgar's gravesite not only humbled me but empowered me. I felt fragile yet very significant. My existence mattered immensely but in much different ways than I had been experiencing. I had a lot to learn and accomplish, but I had met a milestone. I drove the rest of the way home to Kansas.

We began harvest the day after my sister and I arrived home. It was a bittersweet experience, and a momentous time spent with my family. We cried and shared memories of Kris. This was Kris's wheat. He and Dad had purchased and planted every seed. The wheat had grown to be the most plentiful, golden wheat field that land had produced for us. He loved checking on the wheat, watching the phases of growth, and in Kansas, praying for rain. He appreciated farmers. He appreciated their hard work and dedication to their land and families. He enjoyed the challenge of it all.

Two years before, I had stood on the side of that old John Deere combine with Kris as he meticulously maneuvered the header through the field. Round and round, back and forth. The chaff blew in my face, the cab smelled of faint diesel fuel, the grain sounded like a flowing river as it poured into the truck, and my brother had this huge smile on his face. His laugh was honest. He was the most realistic person I know, so when he laughed, he really laughed. No faking anything in that man's life! On this Kansas land is where he was content. Where he felt most free. In that moment on that combine, he was happy. I was happy. This was his soul's home.

The 2012 harvest was different. Kris was gone. I watched my dad cut the wheat in the same old combine Kris had sat in. I tried to imagine that Kris was proudly watching down on all of us. He was still smiling. I wondered what my dad was thinking about as he made slow rounds in the field. Cutting wheat allows for a lot of time to think while sitting in the cab all alone. Was he longing for his only son?

Each evening when the sun fell behind the horizon, exhausted, we packed up the trucks and headed back into town. While eating our late dinner, we talked about how badly we wished Kris was still with us. All we could do was continue on with our hard work for him, both mentally and physically. What a tribute. What a beautiful way to end the season and close this earthly chapter of Kris's life.

A few days into harvest, in the middle of a hot and windy afternoon in the field, I received a call from a friend in Nashville. She hesitated and said, "I have something to tell you. I just have to tell you because I would want you to tell me. Your husband has been unfaithful to you at least four times."

Adrenaline fired through my veins. I hung up on her and immediately tried calling my husband. I paced frantically up and down a narrow dirt road out by the fields. Not another soul in sight. He didn't answer until the tenth call or so. I knew he had been kayaking with friends on the Harpeth River. That irritated me even more—knowing he was out partying with friends while his wife was learning to live again. He let me drive 13 hours, grieving, knowing he had done me so wrong, in so many ways.

I demanded he tell me everything. I told him he owed me at least that much. He admitted it all. There was no reason to hide the truth any longer. My heart beat through my entire body. I remembered where I was at the time of the described events. Betrayal. I called him every single name under the Kansas sun, repeating each just to make sure his ears would bleed the words for the rest of his earthly existence. It would have been different if we had been divorcing or had been separated. I didn't realize our relationship had slipped *this* far. I was totally blind-sided. We were still living together and sleeping together. His infidelity began before Kris passed away and continued after. The pain was unbearable. My heart hurt so bad. Just a few months earlier I had lost my brother, now I was losing my husband. I knew my marriage was not healthy. I knew I was not a happy wife. I knew my family had turmoil. I was absolutely miserable, but this was unfathomable. I had been loyal; I would have been loyal till my dying breath. I took a vow; I meant those vows. I married for life.

I slept with my sister that night and bawled my eyes out. The pain radiated through my chest and throat, through my bones. My entire body ached. To make matters worse, the next day was Memorial Day. I had to go out to my brother's gravesite for the first time since we'd buried him and see other people from the church. The Mennonite church. We weren't going to attend their Memorial Day service, but we wanted to go to Kris's gravesite as a family.

The Mennonite denomination is a very strict and conservative Christian sect. My parents were both raised in the church, and all of my extended family is Mennonite. They are good people, but there has always been a palpable distance between them and us, the non-members. Now here I was, with a brother who had taken his own life and a marriage fumbling towards divorce. My family, the black sheep. Me, now the blackest sheep of all. Mennonites certainly frown upon suicide and divorce, and they sure have a one-way-ticket-to-hell viewpoint on both circumstances. I felt judged. I wanted to stick up for Kris. I wanted them to understand the depth of his situation and the pain he experienced. A lot of them did know him and would agree that he was a good man, but the act of suicide can bring forth a lot of damning judgment. It certainly is hard to justify what he did, but I wanted to offer a broader perspective and an open mind to other beliefs and opinions. I didn't want Kris to be judged any longer. I wanted compassion instead of religious dogma. I wanted forgiveness instead of judgment. I wanted understanding instead of denial. I wanted them to know the truth.

While standing by my brother's freshly dug grave, I thought of my current situation with my husband, and I wanted to crawl into a dark hole. Yet another challenge had stepped in front of me. I was numb, and nothing felt real. I anticipated the future shame I would experience as my friends and the community heard the news about my divorce. I feared the difficult decisions I would have to face and the permanent stigma of being a divorced woman. My head was in a fog. We spent just enough time paying respects at the gravesite and then drove home.

The next few days were a blur. We finished up the harvest, yet I continued to live in an emotional prison. I feared my future so much; I called my husband repeatedly and said things like, "We just need to get away. I love you. Things will get better. Let's work this out. Remember all the good times? We're meant to be, this isn't right. What do I need to do?"

This may seem completely crazy for a woman to say after being in an unhealthy marriage, but as I found out, it's very common. I was so scared of a future without him, a future that felt so uncertain. I was afraid to be a divorced woman, afraid I was too old to find love again. At that time I would have done anything to preserve my marriage. I clung to it in the wake of losing Kris. Looking back now, I know our relationship had to end at that time, and deep down my subconscious knew that was best for us as well. My husband had clocked out. He was not fit to help me grieve. I also couldn't be the wife I needed to be for him during the process of trying to find my true self. We were not fit for each other any longer. He had himself to worry about. He didn't know how to support me through the roughest time in my life, and I didn't know how to help him help me. He emotionally detached from his grieving wife. I detached from him. Love was no longer there to hold us together. Even the idea of love was gone. We were over.

I spent a few weeks with my family. We all needed each other. It was the best place I could be, but depression set in. It greeted me with angry force every morning I woke up. Getting out of bed was misery; breathing was misery. My brother's trucks were outside, and his clothes, books, furniture, camping gear, and all of his belongings were piled up in the garage. I had to walk past his things every day, and it was all just too much—sleeping in the same room I grew up in, with the stuffed animals from my childhood, and the track and tennis medals on the wall. The same basement smell, the coolness of my room. The northern gusts of wind striking my dugout windowpane. In the mornings, the same stream of sunshine cast a warm glow onto my carpet. This was the room Kris and I slept in on Christmas Eve as children, discussing with immense anticipation what gifts Santa was going to bring us that night. As safe as home felt, the memories haunted me. They took me back to days of innocence, opportunity, success, and joy—when I didn't know this kind of sorrow.

My response was to get away. I wasn't trying to run away, but I needed something more, something new, something bigger. A change. A push in the direction toward healing. I needed to be inspired. I craved being near the ocean. I researched retreats online and found one in California at a good price. A week later, I was on a plane to Laguna Beach. Here I received counseling every day and lots of support for a week. It was amazing, it was beneficial, but it didn't fix me. I didn't really expect it to, but I needed a change of scenery and a healthy dose of hope and advice. I had great conversation with people I met, and they encircled me with empathy and compassion. They also shared their stories of heartache and loss with me. The program director had lost her 18-year-old son to suicide, so I connected with her. In those moments, I knew I was at the right place at the right time. The retreat allowed me to regain some of my independence and identity, but I still had a long way to go on the journey to health and emotional freedom. I took walks along the beach, and I journaled each day. My family checked in on me to make sure I was all right. One morning my dad texted me a poem he had found in a book. In any situation I always wanted my dad's approval, his blessing, and his support.

When I received this poem, I knew he was going to stand by my side through this divorce and offer the loving strength I had hoped for. Here is the poem he sent me, written by Lucy Larcom:

*Is it raining little flower? Be glad*
*of rain; too much sun would*
*wither thee; twill shine again.*
*The clouds are very black, tis*
*true; but just behind them shines*
*the blue. Art thou weary tender*
*heart? Be glad of pain; in sorrow*
*sweetest virtues grow, as flowers*
*in the rain. God watches, and*
*thou wilt have sun, when clouds*
*their perfect work have done.*

I wrote down another quote while at the retreat, this one by Jerry Sittser:

*The quickest way for anyone to*
*reach the sun and the light of day*
*is not to run west, chasing after the*
*setting sun, but to head east,*
*plunging into the darkness until*
*one comes to the sunrise.*

I related to this quote. I believed every word of it. It was symbolic of where I was at that point. I was plunging into the void to find myself, to grow, to learn, to meet unexpected challenges head on. I didn't have to avoid that darkness; I didn't have to be afraid. To truly heal, I had to face the unknown. At some point I would reach the other side with the sun rising up over the horizon, greeting me with a brand new day and a brand new life.

In Laguna Beach, I had a burning desire to find myself again. I needed to find out who Misty was outside of her marriage. I needed to find out who that girl was before she'd plunged into love with that man at 23 years old. I wanted her back. I wanted to find that girl and start a new life. I wanted to dig deep into my grief, dissect my emotions, clear a path, and begin again. I had blind faith of a better life ahead, and the desire to find it fueled me onward with no inhibitions. I was determined to clear my mental clutter and own my happiness—even without my brother on this earth, even without my husband in my life. I wanted to regain control of my future; it was possible.

I returned to Kansas with the intention to keep moving forward. I needed to get back to Nashville, start applying some of the things I'd learned, and face my new reality and my divorce. My sister and Mom drove the 13 hours down to Nashville with me. I feared walking into my cold and abandoned home, which I hadn't been inside in weeks. My husband had moved out. He'd already attempted to run away from this reality of a broken marriage. Pet sitters were taking care of Munkee, our tuxedo cat, and Zoe, our golden retriever. Our pets were used to us being around, in and out of the house every day. Then suddenly their lives changed too. I missed them. When we pulled up in the drive, Zoe's head popped up over the backyard gate. She was skinny, yet her tail was still wagging. I was sad. But a dog is always forgiving. She was happy I was home. My cat hesitatingly greeted me at the back door, slight fear in his eyes. I held him and said, "I'm sorry." He soon forgave my absence and rubbed up against my leg.

I never dreamed that when I left for Kansas a month earlier, I would be facing this indescribable challenge. A part of me thought I would leave for a week, cut the wheat, refuel, be with family, gain some clarity, offer myself and my husband a break, and somehow return to a better life. Instead, I returned to a house that reeked of deep abandonment. Memories flooded through my mind. The good. The bad. The betrayal. Sadness and emptiness hung in the air like a thick fog. It was as if nobody had lived there in years. An echo danced through the rooms. My plants were lifeless. My husband had cleaned out his office, and all that remained were photos of us on the walls. I walked through the house like a ghost. The small purple room would have been our first baby's nursery. I could still picture Kris working so hard to tile our bonus room. Out in the yard, weeds had taken over the fenced-off garden that my husband and I had tended together. This house held our dreams, our laughter, our anger, the distance between us, and the secrets he kept from me.

So what did we do? We cleaned … or my mom and sister did anyway. That was their first instinct to begin helping me through this. While I walked the house in circles, trying to comprehend my reality, they watered the drooping plants, swept the floor, opened the curtains, rearranged furniture, washed the sheets, took my wedding photos off the walls, and saged the house to clear that thick, hurtful emotional air. They didn't shed a tear. They stayed positive and kept moving forward. They were there for me when I broke down, they listened, and they held me when I was weak. I know they were hurting inside, as they, too, were losing yet another person in their lives. But we were now a team. When one person is down, the others help pick you up, knowing that each of you will fall at some point. This divorce was another major change, another turn in the path, another heartache for all of us. We had strength between us. It was time to keep moving on with blind faith. That night my mom and I slept on an air mattress in my husband's barren office. I couldn't bear to sleep in the same bedroom or bed that I'd slept in with him for five married years.

My mother and I have always had a great relationship, just as she has had with her other children. She is the epitome of goodness. She exemplifies the definition of patience. Her empathetic heart is plated with forgiveness and love. A complaining word has never touched her tongue, and she always sees the good in people. Survival drives her instincts. We share a connection that cannot be described. She is not only a mother, she is a friend. She offers support and strength through just her presence. She's a tender woman who loves the beauty of flowers, the early morning hours, conversation over coffee, the adventure of travel, and who will always have a strong desire to learn, to grow, and to be better than the day before. The loss of her son affected her in much the same way his death affected me. It lit within her an urge to be better, a desire to help. She is a soft-spoken woman, and she is my rock. She did not fail me throughout the process of losing my husband.

My sister was also a rock. A best friend. Someone who would do anything for anyone. She's a compassionate woman, a lover of nature, a creative soul with acute attention to detail. She's always the one to give the most thoughtful gifts with the prettiest paper and the cute handmade finishing touches. There's not a selfish bone in her body. We've been great friends since I was fifteen years old. Her junior by five years, I had to grow up to meet her approval. That's just how it goes, and I was honored to finally join her club. She gets me. I get her. My sister knows everything about me, and it feels good to be in the presence of someone who loves you for who you truly are. She has no judgments, no motives, no secrets. We have a mutual respect for one another, regardless of the situation, and share the same sense of humor, just as we did with Kris. The three of us could have a good time doing anything or nothing. Some of the best times in my life have been with my sister and brother. Each of us knew what the others were thinking without saying a word. The hardest I've laughed has been when the three of us were together, and especially when my dad offered his two cents of dry humor as well. Things weren't always perfect, but there was a bond between us five that could not be broken. Eckhart Tolle says, "Being present for someone with no expectations and wanting is what true love is." This is my family, and they were all proving their love in those moments leading up to the divorce process.

The next morning, the three of us girls awoke to a banging on my front door. We all knew what it was. I was being served divorce papers. With my hair a mess and brain in a fog, I took the papers from the stone-faced woman at the door. I had anticipated that moment, but it still hurt. Somehow though, the papers in my hands also signified the beginning of a fight. The fight for my new life. I now had serious work to do.

The next few months were filled with emails, paperwork, and meetings with my attorney. I dreaded going to my PO box every day to retrieve more heart-wrenching mail. I just wanted it all to end. I wanted the burden lifted so I could finally begin rebuilding my life. The divorce process took almost a year. I had absolutely no idea it would take that long. We did not have kids, but we did have some assets to settle. It was heartbreaking to say the least. At one time, we'd been best friends, and now it seemed we hated each other with every fiber of our being and fought tooth and nail. Through all the mud slinging, defensiveness, and attorney bickering, I developed a hard shell. I again became someone I temporarily didn't know. For my own well-being, I had to remind myself of my emotional choices. Instead of assuming the world was out to get me, I had to learn to process anger, jealousy, and insecurity.

I made it a point to not date for a year. I needed that year to heal my heart. The last thing I wanted or needed was to get mixed up with the wrong guy, someone to fix me, or someone for me to fix. Even though it felt like my emotional and physical needs were unmet at that time, I needed time alone to work on me and only me. Also, I needed time to process my grief. A divorce can be similar to a death in that you are grieving the loss of someone in your life. Even if you aren't in love with that person anymore, or know that it is for the best to not be together, it's still a major life change that requires letting go of that person and the past. That person still exists physically, and that can bring on its own amount of emotional turmoil as well because you know he or she is also moving on with his or her own life. Jealousy, anger, and resentments can come up. I wrote about these emotional struggles. I also wrote about what I wanted, needed, and deserved. I needed to feel loved in a way that maybe I'd never known before. I needed to trust someone. I wanted to feel special and attractive again. I suppose I just wanted to feel, period.

Luckily, new people, experiences, and opportunities presented themselves to me. I met amazing new friends, huge catalysts to progress in my life. I knew these people would be close to me forever. It was refreshing to meet new people who knew me outside of my marriage and had never known my soon-to-be ex-husband. I reclaimed my identity. I took opportunities to travel to new cities, and life became fun again. I was growing into an independent, single woman who loved whom she was becoming.

Though it was pushed back three times, mediation day finally came. I was so relieved. Going into it, I felt pretty good. I was confident, ready to settle our assets, and ready to finalize the divorce. We took our positions in separate rooms, and the mediator went back and forth hearing our sides. It was a painful fight to say the least. Finally, after six hours, it was over. All was settled. There was nothing else to do but go home. So I went back to an empty, quiet house—the house where my ex and I had once began our life together. I lay on my bed and cried my final tears of grief for my marriage and the life I had anticipated.

As hard as that day was, it signified official closure and freedom. It was all necessary, and I was proud of myself. I had made my home my own. The simplest things made a huge difference. I'd rearranged the rooms and added color. My house felt light and cheery—completely different from a year ago. The purple room was my office. I had photos of new friends in my picture frames. My bookshelves held my books and Kris's beloved books. The past memories of my house were healed.

A couple of nights after mediation, I had a very vivid and meaningful dream: I walk upon a large plateau by myself. There isn't another manmade structure in sight. Just a large vista, like a painting, surrounds me. It is as if

I am at the edge of the world, looking over the massiveness of eternity. The colors are dynamic and alive. Shades of orange, red, yellow, and gold glisten across the landscape. I look over the horizon. A sliver of an orange sun rises up over the earth. I am in awe. I walk to the edge of the plateau and sit with my legs hanging down over the cliff. The sun slowly rises. My heart and soul expand with the grandeur and beauty.

When I awoke, I immediately related the dream to the quote by Jerry Sittser that I had written down in my quote journal while in Laguna Beach. This dream signified a major milestone. I had trudged and traveled through the dark void over the last year and was able to finally see my life in full color. I was looking forward to rebuilding. On March 20th, the paperwork to finalize the divorce was complete; it was the first day of spring, my favorite season.

*If we had no winter, the spring would not be so pleasant; if we did not sometimes taste of adversity, prosperity would not be so welcome.*

—ANNE BRADSTREET

# CHAPTER THREE

# My dad

The first Christmas without Kris and my husband, my family felt the need to do something different from our traditional Christmas at home in Kansas. The Colorado mountains have always been a place of refuge and joy for us, so we gathered in Golden, Colorado. We stayed at a hotel just a few blocks from downtown. The landscape had just received a peaceful blanket of snowfall, and the streets were decorated with lights. We had our Christmas dinner at the hotel restaurant and opened presents in front of the fireplace in my parents' comfy hotel room. My favorite gift was a wind chime. My eyes teared up when I saw it. I knew my mother understood the significance of that chime. She'd bought one for herself too. I couldn't wait to hang it on my back porch and listen to its song in Tennessee, another reminder of Kris's presence.

We went ice skating, toured the Coors brewery, and strolled through downtown Boulder. My sister and I pretended to perform a concert on the Red Rocks stage. We were all able to relax and laugh for a few days and not dwell on the sadness of our loss. But despite the laughs, one thing that was very evident was Dad's decline in health. His breath was short, his heart would race, his energy was low. He was losing weight. When he tried to sleep, he would wake in a panic. He was so low on sleep. He attempted to keep up with us, but by the end of our trip, we were all very concerned. My sister and I had planned to fly back to our homes on the fourth day of the trip, but we cancelled our flights so we could drive back to Kansas with our parents. We needed to make sure Dad was going to be okay, and we planned to get him to the hospital when we got home. All of our luggage barely fit into their car, but we packed it in tight and drove to my parents' house.

That night my sister and I slept on a bed of blankets on the floor next to Dad. He woke up every 30 minutes and had a panic attack. My sister and I would get up and try to calm him down. The next morning we demanded to take him to the doctor.

His doctor checked his heart rate and admitted him into the ICU immediately. In a way, we were thankful because we were not capable of or comfortable caring for him anymore; we needed him in a safe and controlled environment. We spent New Year's Eve in the hospital room with my dad. They kept him for about four days to stabilize his heart rate and run tests, and he was diagnosed with atrial fibrillation. This was the beginning of yet another challenge. My mountain was getting steeper.

A few days later I felt comfortable enough to fly back to Nashville. I knew he wasn't well, but I trusted the doctors and planned to return for a visit after mediation, which was scheduled for January 16th.

I had been back in Nashville for about ten days when, on January 15th, I received a call from my mother. Dad was being taken by heart ambulance to Wichita. He had seen his doctor, who advised him to see a heart specialist immediately. With mediation scheduled for the next morning, I was under instant stress. I had been anticipating that day for many months and I had to make a quick decision as to what to do. I contacted my paralegal and attorney about the situation, and with their support, I knew it was best to book a flight to Kansas. Much to my dismay, mediation got re-scheduled for two months later, March 14th. The burden of the divorce seemed it would never lift, but I knew my dad needed me. I didn't want any more regrets.

I ended up spending another week in the hospital with my dad. He had to have surgery to remove 4.5 liters of fluid from his lungs. We all had high hopes that the surgery would help him regain his ability to breath better, stabilize his heart rate, and have more energy. He seemed a bit better, yet he still was not completely well. He was still having a hard time gaining his weight back. They put him on blood thinners that he had to take in precise amounts to minimize the risk of a stroke. A few days after his surgery, my dad went back home, and once again I flew back to Nashville.

Through all of this, my mom was overwhelmed. She had a shop to run, a house to keep, and more responsibilities than normal due to Dad's inability to work as hard as he once did. She needed to get away for a little while. So, once mediation day came and went, and she felt Dad was stable, she came to visit me. She enjoyed my house as a refuge. We were excited to spend some good quality time together, with me as a newly single woman, and a lot of hardships now in our past.

The first evening she was in Nashville, we went to see Kris Kristofferson at the Ryman. We've loved his music for years, and my brother was named in his honor. My mom and I laughed, we cried, and we reminisced as we watched him perform. After the show, we were just outside the venue when we got a call from my sister telling us that something was wrong with Dad. She had been on the phone with him just minutes earlier and his words were making no sense. She could only hear a jumbled mess of unrecognizable sounds. She said he sounded panicked. An ambulance was on its way to my parents' house. The doctor called us an hour later and confirmed that my father had had a stroke. In shock, Mom and I booked the first early morning flight back to Kansas.

There was no blood on Dad's brain and the stroke mainly affected his speech and the right side of his body. He was not talking. He could comprehend, yet he couldn't form words. Absolutely horrifying. Just the day before, I was so joyful and grateful to be able to spend a few days with my mother. Then suddenly, I was questioning so much again. I felt guilty for allowing Mom to come see me. I could only imagine how she felt. I couldn't stand the thought of my dad feeling trapped, unable to express himself. He didn't deserve yet another challenge. He had just lost his best friend and only son. What more was going to be taken from him?

I would ask *why*, and then I would ask myself *Who am I asking why?* Am I talking to a white-bearded man in the sky who is punishing us? Am I asking the universe? Am I asking myself? I didn't even know. Emotions overlapped once again. It would have been easy to feel like a victim. I had to trust that everything would get better. Other challenges in my life had transformed into a better experience. I had to learn to process the circumstances. I had to let go of my regrets. It was easy to blame myself, just as I did after Kris passed and my marriage failed. But regrets would ultimately hold me back. I had to keep climbing. This was certainly another obstacle on my path, but I was stronger and wiser than I'd ever been.

Dad eventually got transferred to a rehabilitation unit in Wichita. He still was not speaking, although he did understand most everything we said. Since the stroke affected the left side of his brain, he had limited use of his right arm and hand. We worked with him daily in physical therapy and speech therapy for a couple of weeks. He wanted desperately to communicate words to us, but he couldn't get the words out. Only sounds. He was able to make facial expressions, and his eyes looked bright and alert. But he was not the dad I'd watched work a wheat field just a year ago. He was supposed to be strong, witty, wise, and active. Now I had to wipe food off his mouth when he ate. I had to help him get dressed. He was no longer physically strong. He was 40 pounds underweight. All I could do was be there for him and reassure him all would be well. Truth was I didn't know what the outcome was going to be.

The questions flooded my mind daily. What is the meaning for all these tragedies in my life? Is there a meaning? Have we not learned the lessons? When we learn the lessons will things get better? Is life just what it is? No outside force, no reason? I thought I had things figured out, but obviously I was still learning.

I had a lot of time to think while sitting in the chair next to Dad's hospital bed. I watched him sleep and thought of the dad I knew growing up. He was the one we would go to for the big answers, for the support, for the strength to carry on. He was a builder. He was a fixer. A perfectionist. He was smart, he was intuitive. His hobbies included collecting historic artifacts, specifically Civil War memorabilia. His humor was dry, and he didn't speak just to speak. When he spoke, his words came from his heart and with conviction. He was the foundation of our family. He was a man of quiet confidence and a keen instinct. A hard-working man who supported his family and protected them with the sharp look of an eye.

I thought back to a moment with my dad when I was five years old. I lay on a blanket in the grass in the back yard with him. It was nighttime. We lay there contently staring up at the stars and moon. It was a spontaneous event, and I was up later than usual, which also made it feel important. I felt so special in that moment. I don't remember many words exchanged. Just Dad and me, on a blanket, looking at the night sky in wonderment. We pointed out the brightest stars. I had the same curiosity and amazement at five years old as I do as an adult. Everything was okay. I remember the smile in my heart as we shared a quiet moment in the summer air that night. The most simplistic moments can often be the most powerful. And those moments with my dad laying in silence beside me in his hospital bed were no different. The connection we had as a father and daughter was still there. No different from when I was five years old.

My dad's speech did not come back. He still couldn't connect sounds to complete an identifiable word.

Although slower than normal, he was able to regain most of his range of motion and walking skills. He was able, once again, to eat on his own and dress himself. We were thankful for these accomplishments. Yet the loss of the vocal communication between us made me feel as if I was losing yet another man in my life. The loss of Kris was always at the forefront of my thoughts as a true example of how quickly someone can be taken away from us. I was afraid of losing my dad completely. Slowly, one by one, the most important male figures in my life were leaving me. I tried not to take one moment for granted with my dad. But once again, as a family we had to learn to live differently.

Now Dad needed us to provide strength and encouragement for him. My sister, Mom, and I had to stick together and also offer strength and support to one another. We finally received clearance from the doctors for Dad to return home. They suggested that he continue speech and physical therapy. We were forced to live a foreign way of life that didn't offer a road map or any kind of rules, and certainly no guarantees.

After returning to Nashville, I tried to get back to Kansas every couple of months to help out at home. Throughout the months, Dad worked hard and regained his ability to write. The words weren't always spelled correctly, but we were incredibly grateful for his ability to piece some words and sentences together on paper. We communicated by way of his writing, and we also relied a lot on his facial expressions and hand gestures to understand what he was telling us. My dad had previously always been in control of his life and his circumstances, but he was suddenly faced with something very much out of his control. I can't say he was very welcoming to this change. He was a fairly simple, small-town, Midwestern farm guy. We had to remind him to bring his little notepad and pen with him wherever he went, though he wanted to believe he could still communicate otherwise. We all learned to adapt as best we could, but it was not easy. Patience did run thin on both sides, and I had to step back and regain perspective and be thankful that my dad was even still there at all. He could have been paralyzed, he could not know who I am, he could have died. Although his physical strength had been weakened, his mental strength was still there. His spirit was the same, and he still loved us as a father should. Love wasn't only expressed verbally. Love was shown through the look of an eye, the touch of a hand, the gift of an act, through the power of a hug, and misspelled words on the back of a steakhouse receipt.

As events beyond our control caused shifts in our lives, we had to learn to do things we never anticipated. For one thing, the chores Kris used to help Dad with became partly us girls' responsibility. Dad wanted us to be a part of what he and Kris loved and worked on together. Vehicles, machines, and property had to continue to be maintained. We had tough decisions to make, we had work that needed to be done. We tried to fill Kris's shoes, but we quickly realized that was absolutely impossible. We could only be the best version of ourselves, and we certainly had our laughs while trying to wear the different hats that Dad asked us to try on. My sister and I had never imagined being arms deep in an old combine or tractor engine, but we did what we had to do.

I had a choice to continue to either work hard at healing or get knocked down by the circumstances. Some days I had to let myself be sad, mad, or regretful. I had my days of waking up in a cloud of emotion, reliving the phone call from my sister the night Kris died, that day in the wheat field when I found out my marriage was ultimately over, and the moment outside the Ryman when I found out about my dad's stroke. Those memories of my heart sinking to the floor were always just a thought away. There were many days when I didn't know if I needed to focus on the grief of losing my brother, my husband, communication with my dad, my sudden change in career path, the fear about my future, or all of the above. I dissected the issues in my marriage to recognize and understand my unhealthy habits and patterns. I wanted to be a better person for going through that relationship. As for my brother, I wanted to keep his memory and spirit close to me in a positive manner. In other words, any negative memories of my ex-husband could be eliminated from my future life, and my brother's positive memory could remain. It was completely up to me. All the while, I was trying to find meaning within the circumstances of my dad's stroke. I thought maybe the situation could strengthen my relationship with my dad or allow for other opportunities of growth. I had to assume there were blessings within it.

We have no control over the permanence of situations or people in our lives. Life is a process of letting go—letting go of what we maybe once had, what we think we should have, material things, the physical nature of the ones we love, and our regrets. I had more to learn. I was not giving up. I could see the mountain peak.

*If the stars should appear but one night every thousand years how man would marvel and stare.*

—RALPH WALDO EMERSON

# CHAPTER FOUR

# St. John

In February of 2013, on a whim I applied for a 30-day work exchange program at an eco-resort in St. John, USVI. I had a gnawing desire for an adventure, some time away to mark the end of a long, grueling challenge. I was single and capable. Now was the time to step outside of my comfort zone and challenge myself in new ways. In exchange for lodging, I'd work five hours a day, five days a week. To my surprise, I was accepted and was asked to go down to the island for the month of July. A couple of months after my acceptance, my dad had his stroke, so I battled with whether or not to go after all, because I didn't want to be selfish. I worried about my family. When I discussed the opportunity with my parents, they were 100 percent supportive. My dad knew I needed this adventure. It was a chance of a lifetime. So I started saving my money and booked my flights. I trusted that I would gain more than I ever expected from going away for a month. At the time I really didn't know what that meant, but I trusted that something great was possible.

There were other deep reasons why I wanted to go back to the island. First of all, I felt guilt for having been there while Kris was fighting for his life. Second, my ex-husband and I had spent two vacations in St. John. I wanted to make the island "mine" again. As I did with my house, I wanted to create new memories, all on my own. I didn't want my memories of the island to be clouded by sadness or regrets. Overall, I wanted to experience what the top of my mountain would feel like.

I flew down to the island where I didn't know a soul. I arrived on July 2nd, one day before my brother's 30th birthday. My suitcase was not as lucky, as it ended up lost somewhere between Nashville and St. Thomas. I slept in my clothes that night and wondered what the heck I was doing. I was already nervous I had made a mistake. Luckily I was reunited with my huge red suitcase the following afternoon and quickly grounded myself into the island environment.

I celebrated Kris's birthday hiking and relaxing on the beach, cherishing memories of him and me. My intention was that the trip would offer a renewed relationship with him, a mental and physical challenge for me, a final reclamation of myself and my happiness, and hopefully even more.

The resort was located on the remote side of the island. I stayed in a small, minimally furnished solar-powered eco tent. The tents stood on stilts, like tree houses, on the side of a cliff overlooking the Caribbean ocean. It was secluded, and I loved it. Each wall of the structure had large screens covered by canvas that I could unzip for fresh air. The floors were unfinished concrete. I slept in a small bed similar to a cot. I had a propane stove and a small refrigerator. The solar-powered lights were dim, so I always had a flashlight near. My tent was the farthest from the main office and cafe. All tents and main areas of the resort were connected by tall, narrow, wooden walkways, also on stilts. Access to anywhere required many, many steps. It was hot. It was humid. No need to do your hair or put on makeup. I learned quickly to adapt to my environment and the climate. Didn't really need that huge red suitcase after all! I really ended up living out of a backpack. No blow dryer, no hair straightener, no curling iron. Just shower and go.

At night it was pitch dark. I fell asleep to the crashing sea and the boisterous song of the tree frogs. The latch on my tent door was broken, and I chose to not get it fixed. For some reason I challenged myself to be fearless and find security in the thoughts in my mind. I am safe, I told myself.

I bathed in a partially exposed wooden shower with solar-heated water from a big black barrel. The water fed from a manually operated garden hose. I had no TV, no internet, and no phone service. It was a challenge, and I loved it. I read and wrote each night. I awoke at 4:30 a.m., opened up the outdoor cafe, and greeted and served the breakfast guests. The turquoise water of Salt Pond Bay was in clear view from my work. So beautiful. Some evenings my new friends and I would grill out by the pool that was centrally located within the small resort. We laughed. We connected. We drank cheap coconut rum and learned from one another. We each had a reason to be there.

Almost every evening I would hike a half mile uphill to get phone service to call or text home to see how my family was doing. Thankfully, my dad maintained his health while I was gone. His speech did not get any better, but his writing continued to improve, which helped us immensely to communicate. I had come a long way with processing and healing the grieving wounds of my brother and husband. My dad was my new focus. This was not a problem I needed to necessarily fix, it was something I needed to nurture. It was a relationship that I needed to hold close to my heart. Things can change in the blink of an eye, so it became very important to me to cherish those people who love me regardless of how messy my life gets.

My 30 days away challenged me. I was disconnected from cell phone service, the internet, and social media outlets. Without these distractions, I was forced to look inward even more. I had my own thoughts to face. My own voice to hear. My own life to contemplate. Beyond that, the hot, humid environment—combined with lots of steps, no air conditioning, and no vehicle—offered physical and mental challenges that were, in fact, liberating and fulfilling. Going to the island without knowing anyone was another challenge, one which helped me gain even more independence and helped me to understand and experience the freedom of making my own decisions every day. Nobody else was present to resist, encourage, or control my actions. I was responsible for how my day turned out. Only me. This also was incredibly liberating.

I was able to put into perspective my marriage and divorce. It had all seemed so complicated—the reasons for the dissolution of our union. Yet I was able to learn a lot of valuable lessons from the pain and experience. I surrendered to my faults. I took responsibility for the times I failed and I forgave myself. I held no grudges against my ex-husband. I chose to not bear hurtful memories of the past. The gratitude I felt for my growth far out-weighed any burden of regret or grudge. The maturity I experienced because of my marriage and divorce allowed me the opportunity to recognize what I truly need in relationships going forward. I knew myself better than I ever had before—and for this reason there was no shame of my past. Marriage is a selfless commitment to another person. There should be no expectation of an equivalent return on your efforts, although if you are in in the right union, that is exactly what you will receive. Of course, one must love and know him or herself first and foremost, but if each person gives 100 percent with the other in mind first, each will receive what they need. Isn't that how it should work? I also learned how to be open and honest. I found redemption in opening up to the world around me and letting people into my life in a deeper and more meaningful way. I was stronger than I ever knew, and my divorce helped me prove that.

I also learned that I *was* kind-of a morning person. Who knew? Well honestly, getting up at 4:30 a.m. five days a week was not my favorite part, but the sunrises made it all worth the initial grogginess of waking that early for work. About a quarter mile from my tent, there was a bench at the edge of the eastern cliff. I didn't go every morning, maybe two or three times a week. But each time I went, I was alone. All quiet, with not a soul in sight. When I first arrived, there was darkness. Then just as anticipated, the sun showed its bright colors behind the massiveness of the ocean. There was nothing to do but stare in awe and complete, submissive respect. Respect for nature, for God, for beauty, for life. The miracle of a brand new day.

My trip to the island allowed me to think, reflect, and heal the remaining wounds on my heart. I was able to let go completely. The ocean was healing and encouraged a feeling of freedom that I didn't know existed. It made me feel alive. In those still moments by the water, I realized that nothing in the world could destroy my happiness. Pure happiness is something that lies deep within the soul.

Nobody can take that from me, or you. We fight for our happiness. We create our own happiness. It is ours to keep, as long as we want it. I had finally found my joy.

I also found myself within necessary moments of breakdown. Moments of pure, deep, honest emotion. One evening, while on my hike back through the woods from the beach, Kris was on my mind. His presence was strong. I felt so grateful for how far I had come. I was humbled by my experience and knew there was a purpose for everything. But I missed him. I had focused so much on maintaining my strength through the hardships that I failed to let myself be vulnerable and emotional. Strength had become my coping mechanism.

On my hike back that evening I let myself melt. I thought of Kris's smile. His laugh. His honest eyes. His pain. It rained. I cried. I laid my head against a tree while the rain poured off my back. The rain and my tears hit the ground in tandem. I felt touched by the moment. It was a release. It was love—an overwhelming expression of so much love for my brother that no words can properly express. Only tears. It was okay to cry. No matter how well healed, how far I was up the mountain, or how strong I wanted to be, I would always have the need to cry—to be vulnerable. There was nobody else on the trail, and I wouldn't have cared if there was. I needed in that moment to allow myself to express my grief, which I know will always be a part of me. I will not always be broken, but being human means I will always miss my brother. I was learning to live in a healthy companionship with this newly evolved grief. It no longer felt angry and defeating. Yes, I will forever wonder what it would have been like to see Kris grow older, wonder what kind of husband and father he could have become. I will always wonder why he couldn't figure it out and what I could have done differently to help. But the good thing is, I can always find my brother in the woods. And that is the peace I need to move on to another day. I was so thankful for my realizations and resolutions. I had finally cleared my path in order to begin again.

As I approached the end of my trip, I had grown into my happiness. I realized that I may not always be on a beautiful tropical island, but I could take that feeling of happiness with me anywhere. *That* is the feeling I was determined to strive for and find back in Laguna Beach. Every step up that mountain, every tear I cried, every sleepless night, and every moment of doubt was worth it. I felt freedom from the past, contentment for my present moment, and excitement for my future. There was fire behind my soul, an encouraging force of life. A good life. So very good.

I returned to Nashville on August 2nd. Not only did I return with a smile, I also returned with a really smelly backpack and a really nice tan! The next morning, I packed up my car with Zoe and Munkee and drove to Kansas to see my parents. It was surreal to be driving through the plains only 24 hours after having spent 30 days on an island. But I was glad to return to a reality that I loved—a reality that helped make me who I was, and who I was becoming. My family had become a yoked team, with the common goal of happiness. We became fighters and survivors. I was incredibly grateful for my last couple of years. I neither imagined I would experience such a crisis or feel the relieve that comes with it. I never dreamed that such a truly painful journey of loss could lead me down roads that offered the opportunity for me to expand. To find myself. To be the best of me. To become aware of the open door to the birdcage. To fly.

*Sometimes you find yourself in the middle of nowhere, and sometimes in the middle of nowhere is where you find yourself.*

—Unknown

# CHAPTER FIVE

# **Grief**

According to Webster's Dictionary, grief is:
1. *Deep sorrow, esp. that caused by someone's death.*
2. *Trouble or annoyance.*
3. *Deep mental anguish, as that arising from bereavement.*

This is definitely an accurate description, but in no way does it begin to describe the massiveness and complexity of the emotion and the experience it brings forth. My definition of grief reads more like this...

*An overwhelming, crushing, suffocating force that abruptly, and then continuously, rips your heart out and sucks all the energy from your cells and soul. It then leaves you at the darkest, loneliest, most desolate place in your life, without a hope in the world and zero faith in anyone or anything to pull you through. It makes you feel vulnerable, isolated, confused, exposed, and stripped down to your bare soul, which you suddenly are face to face with in a way you've never known before. The rest of the days ahead look bleak, unnecessary, and unfruitful. Grief may dissipate after some time, but you soon realize it continues to linger in the wings, waiting for another opportunity to attack your mind. Then without warning, it consumes you with its angry force once again. Grief feels angry, it feels resentful, it feels regretful, it feels lonely, it feels unbearably sad, it feels gray, and it feels incredibly un-remorseful.*

Is that accurate? Is that similar to what you're feeling, or have felt? Even these words cannot describe completely how it really feels until it happens to you. The truth is, that painful and angry grief also contains everything that you once loved in someone. It hurts *that* bad because you loved *that* much, and it's just not easy to let go of something you love that much. The love you have for someone has, for a time, been transformed into abandonment and hurt. Instead of understanding, there is a void. You may not recognize it now, but that grief has a purpose, and you cannot get around the difficult emotions it brings. Do not push the grief away, do not ignore it, do not deny it. Your grief will be the most overwhelming and significant part of your journey. Feel it, know it, live through it, and eventually it will fade into a better energy and experience. Grief will always be a part of you, but it will transform. The void that you feel now will at some point be filled with love, understanding, and a whole lot of wisdom. It is a process. You must first trust. The emotions that come with a crisis, as complex and complicated as they are, are completely normal, and to be expected. As difficult as a crisis can be to experience, it often can be the catalyst to push you into a richer and more meaningful life.

# CHAPTER SIX

# 24 Truths

*Each truth you learn will be, for you, as new as if it had never been written.*

—Ancient Egyptian Proverb

The following pages contain truths that helped me through my healing process. They are a-ha moments, thoughts, realizations, and activities that really made a difference. My truths were my stepping stones and tools, and they helped me get to the other side of the pain. The other side is where a bright and smiling face came naturally to me. I want this for you too. I want *you* to want this. I want you to feel like you *need* it. At some point after your loss, you should have a strong desire to regain your life. A life where your past does not define you, but has helped shape you into a more inspired and awakened individual. A life that allows you to be proud of where you've been and who you've become. In my opinion, you don't have a choice. You are now faced with the opportunity to see life as an adventure, and challenge yourself to move forward to see what blessings lie ahead.

A common source connects us all. We all love, we all laugh, we all engage, we all hurt, we all have a deeper place within us that wants to be known. This deep, peaceful place is where we will find ourselves. Sometimes a tragedy or a crisis is the start of a whole new beginning. We are not the same people after a major loss; an existential crisis wrapped in grief sends us into a void, a point in our lives where time doesn't exist, where we feel vulnerable and confused. We ask new questions, we feel new emotions, and we see the world differently. We are simply *different*. My hope is that through your losses, you will continue to find yourself—the truest and most honest part of you.

In my first year of grief, I made more progress than I could have ever expected, and four years after my losses, I'm a new person. I can now say that I am who I want and need to be. Now, I'm going to tell you in detail what I did and how I did it. I hope to help give you the strength and encouragement to do the same. If some of these ideas seem foreign, wrong, or impossible to you, that is okay. Please come back to them later, and see if your perspective has changed. Timing is everything, and being patient with yourself is important. These truths aren't necessarily in a specific, sequential order. Your life is precious, important, and well worth the fight. There is a reason you are here. Live your life one day at a time, one moment at a time. Doors will open, light will shine in, and you will feel alive. You too will meet that beautiful, golden sunrise over the plateau.

## *Truth #1*

# *We all have heart scars*

We all suffer losses, which in turn creates what I call "heart scars." Heart scars are memories of pain, memories of losing someone, the sadness of missing someone. But more importantly these scars are also proof of healing and strength. They are marks on our lives that make us who we are. They make us unique, they make us strong, and by acknowledging them we can recognize our humanity, which unites us all. Nobody is immune to the pain of loss. To some degree, loss will undoubtedly be a part of all of our lives.

Again, I know this doesn't make it feel better. For a long time, nothing could justify the loss of my brother or make it hurt less, and nobody could convince me that going through a divorce could offer new opportunities. I'm not trying to justify your loss. But the pain does not last if we don't let it. Wounds want to heal! There is a time to grieve and hurt, and there is also a time to pick yourself up, move on, and regain your life. Be patient, and be thankful when your wounds begin healing to scars. Down the road, those hurtful, grieving wounds will have shaped you.

Embrace who you are, embrace the experiences you have, embrace your wounds. Embrace your humanity, and know you are on a voyage through new territory that leads to invaluable wisdom.

## *Challenge:*

Get yourself a journal. Maybe you buy a nice leather-bound journal from the store or a journal with an inspiring quote or design on the cover. Or maybe you just want to use a plain spiral notebook. Whatever form of paper you want to use is great, but I do suggest it is a book that will stay together and last. In other words, don't use a half used-up notebook from your college days, and don't use loose paper. This journal is going to be an important part of you throughout this journey, and it needs to be somewhat durable. It will be your companion. You may want to look back at your journal for years to come. This is what you will call your life journal.

Once you've got your life journal, begin writing daily or weekly about your grief. Write about your feelings and experiences as you move through your first year of pain. Journaling is a great way to open up to your life experience in a very genuine way. Nobody else needs to read your words, and nobody is judging. Your journal is your companion, your friend. A safe place to land your sorrows. Be honest in your words. No need to hold back. It's okay to feel vulnerable and exposed. It's in our moments of raw emotion that we are often times best able to express our truth. How do you feel?

Draw pictures in your journal. Draw yourself, using symbols, gestures, or stick figures to exemplify where you are at that time in your life. How do you see yourself? Who hurt you? Who do you love? How do you see your position in the grief process? How was your day? What do you desire? If you want, go back after a few months and look at where you were, compared to where you are now. One of the amazing benefits of journaling is the opportunity to go back and see the progress you've made and be proud of your growth. You will have made progress that maybe you didn't even realize.

Two months after losing Kris I drew myself as a stick figure. I sketched fast, as if I needed to place my emotion on the page quickly, to give it an escape from my head. A temporary release. I drew myself as a sad, confused woman, standing on uncertain ground. A woman living in a grey void with an exposed broken heart.

Try doing the same. Translate your experience onto those pages. Your journal will reflect your journey, and your heart scars will be transformed into words and sketches on paper. Be honest, be true. Do not hold back. As hurtful as it can be to feel and express the pain, it is therapeutic. You may have the temptation to resist some thoughts and emotions. It may feel uncomfortable. But it may also feel safe. The longer you journal, the more you will realize it truly is a safe and cathartic experience. We all need an outlet, and your life journal is that tool for you.

*Out of suffering have emerged the strongest souls; the most massive characters are seared with scars.*

—KHALIL GIBRAN

# *Truth #2*

# *Be still*

The night I lost my brother, I demanded for him to let me know where he was. I've never felt such a need to know *where* he was and *how* he was. I needed to save him, help him, hear him, and be with him. Or maybe I needed him to console me. It was terrifying to not understand. This was new to me. A feeling I could have never predicted.

In the initial moments of grief and shock, questions arise that are not conscious. They are automatic and all consuming. But through these thoughts, something kept telling me, *Be still*. I tried. I tried to be still. I tried to listen, but I always found myself anxiously asking again, questioning, wondering, and demanding answers. I wanted some kind of sign that he was still with me. It was too soon to understand exactly *how* to be still.

The day before I left for Kansas, which signified my separation from my husband, was one of the most challenging days of my life. We were each at the end of our respective ropes and couldn't do anything about it. I didn't know about the cheating at the time, but I knew that absolutely nothing about our relationship felt right anymore. I was lost, unstable, and full of fear.

After a long, heart-wrenching conversation with my husband that afternoon while on my lunch break, I told our employees in the office that I had to leave work early that day and that I didn't know if I would be returning, ever. In my mind, I had planned to drive 13 hours to Kansas that afternoon. I had already planned to leave for Kansas a few days later to help my dad cut wheat, but I needed out sooner. The pain was too much. I had to at least temporarily get away from this incredibly painful and unhealthy relationship. Rationally it was a bad idea to leave that afternoon considering my emotional state, my oil change status, and the fact it would be well past 2 a.m. when I got to my parents' house. But I needed out.

So I left work, went home, and lay down in our spare bedroom for a few minutes to think. I was so emotionally exhausted. In that moment, within the silence, I heard in my head a voice again that said, *Misty, be still. Be still and listen.* A calm came over me. I was more in control. With those words in my mind, I could finally place trust in myself, a higher power, and the unknown. I didn't know the answers, but I knew I could find them in my heart if I would just stop thinking and start listening. I then realized that driving that day was not a good idea, so I went for a hike in the woods instead. I took my camera and took photos of nature. It was a beautiful day. I kept telling myself, *Be still and listen.* I walked. I became aware. The sun glistened through the green leaves of the trees. Deer stood peacefully along the trail. The lake rippled and the birds sang. I was finally listening. Being still.

As I walked along the trail, a realization came to me that felt overwhelmingly powerful: *The essence of life is good.* Something bigger and wiser than me offered me this statement. Beyond the pain, beyond the circumstances, beyond what others do to me, beyond the void, life is *good.* It would be okay. As I walked the winding pathway in front of me, I knew there were unknowns. I knew I would stumble. I knew I was facing a painful journey. I also knew that there was understanding to gain and a reason for it all. I finally understood the power of quieting the chatter in my mind, stopping the negativity, and calming the fear. The answers lay in this quiet.

Answers always come in these still moments. I'm thankful for these glimpses of hope and wisdom, but it took me a few months to really be still on a more regular basis. It took some healing time for me to find consistent clarity. My emotional self had to heal before I could realize that this still place is exactly where Kris is, where God is, and ultimately where I am. True comfort and love comes from being still in our thoughts.

## Challenge:

Find your favorite time of the day ... morning, afternoon or evening. During my first year of grief, I felt most connected during the silence of the night. When the sky was dark and the moon shined down, I felt most at peace and connected to my divine guidance. Find that time for you and honor it. Maybe your time is early morning, maybe it's at noon. At least two to three times each week, spend at least 30 minutes in that time of your day, sitting comfortably and reflecting, listening and relaxing. Listen to nature, feel your connection with a higher power or energy, listen to your inner wisdom. Be still. Try to find complete contentment, and feel your soul connect with your natural surroundings. Don't force any thoughts, and don't have expectations. Don't try to figure anything out, don't dwell on the past, don't fear the future. Just be. Feel yourself connected to the trees, to the sun, to the stars, to the moon, to your loved ones, to all that is good. You, too, are an intricate, important piece of this universal cycle. Relax your body, relax your mind. This time is for you to gain mental and emotional strength, wisdom, and clarity.

*For God alone, O my soul, wait in silence, for my hope is from him.*

Psalm 62:5

*Only in quiet waters do things mirror themselves undistorted. Only in a quiet mind is adequate perception of the world.*

—HANS MARGOLIUS

## Truth #3

# Be aware of your emotions

Emotions are a part of being human, and a crucial component to healing throughout our journey. Anger, sadness, fear, jealousy, loneliness—all are completely normal in times of loss. It's inevitable to feel these emotions from time to time, and you may find that they resurface over and over. I felt every emotion possible during my roughest days of grief. When I first heard the news of my brother's death, I felt the emotion physically, as if adrenaline sucked me into a vacuum, a frozen moment where the world stopped turning. This is why my reaction was to run. I wanted to escape that foreign state of being.

My emotions evolved. I shifted from shock to denial quite a few times within the first few weeks and had many moments of denial for months after. I had moments when all I could say over and over was "no, no, no," almost like a chant. I pushed the idea of my brother being gone out of my head before it could even form into a complete thought. It hurt too bad. Then once the reality of the situation crept in, sadness replaced shock. My frozen existence melted. I began to feel. The wounds were wide open, bleeding, and full of pain. So I cried. That's all I knew to do.

Then came anger and depression. During my struggles with depression, sleep was my refuge. All I wanted to do was sleep. When I awoke in the morning, it was as if a sledgehammer hit me in the head with all the heartache. After waking I would think, *How am I supposed to make it through another day?* I can't say that my depressive state lasted too long, mainly because I chose to overcome it. At some point, it was a choice, and my desire for happiness was stronger than my weaknesses. I understand that some people may have an entirely different experience with depression, just as I know my brother did. His depression was chronic, and beyond circumstantial. Mine was certainly due to my losses. I knew I could conquer it, but I had no idea when I would feel better on a regular basis. It was a challenge. It was a fight. I did not give up.

When I felt anger, mostly I felt it towards my husband. I had the choice to let the anger get the best of me or encourage it to dissolve. The anger building up in me was only hurting me. I didn't have too much anger towards my brother. I definitely felt if from time to time, but I would always talk myself through to a position of forgiveness and comfort.

With time and effort, my emotions got easier to manage, and I experienced fleeting glimpses of happiness. Soon enough the joy didn't just last an hour, it lasted four hours, then an entire day. Once I felt this joy and freedom, it was something I knew I wanted more and more of. A lifetime of. Eventually, I accepted, forgave, and let go. I let go of my past sadness, failures, losses, and pain. I realized my losses would always be a significant part of me, but they didn't need to represent my current state of being. I didn't want my past to hold me back. I accepted my divorce. I accepted myself as a divorced woman. I owned that scar and was not ashamed. I forgave the past and my ex-husband. I forgave myself for "failing" at marriage. I was stronger than my adversities. I accepted my brother's death and realized everything I had learned from him and what I had gained due to my experiences of loss. My connection with Kris was stronger than ever once I reached acceptance. I could still smile with him, speak with him, and feel his presence. That was true comfort. I accepted the challenges ahead with my father, knowing I still had a lot be thankful for. I accepted all that had once hurt me. This acceptance was the freedom and growth I had desired and the whole reason for challenging myself in the first place.

Emotions, even painful ones, are natural, normal, and necessary. Feel them, know them, experience them, and allow them to change. Know that this is a process. If you remain stuck in one of these emotional phases, that can be a problem. You should not allow yourself to stay stuck in a negative emotion for too long. Do not stay stuck in denial, anger, depression, sadness, or bargaining. Do not accept those emotions as a part of the rest of your life. Flow through your grieving experience without pushing your way through, as you will need to allow yourself ample time to heal.

Grief is more than an emotion, it is an experience one must process. So do not expect to fix or cure your grief. You will realize at some point that the grief really is love, and that is a manageable existence for your grief.

Again, just because it's healed, doesn't mean the scar doesn't remain. Be patient with yourself, but also know you must progress. Don't let exhausting emotions become a habit or hold you back. Hurtful emotions that linger for too long can become a veil over your life.

## *Challenge:*

One way to stay aware of your emotional state is to practice viewing yourself from an outside perspective. Practice looking at your position from beyond your emotions. When we are immersed in emotions, sometimes it's difficult to see and think clearly. This is the human condition. We are emotional beings, and our emotions allow us to cope, survive, and attempt to control our circumstances and environment, both internal and external. Our emotions allow us to express our experiences, good and bad. We have the capability to examine ourselves, our actions, our patterns, and our lives from an actively objective standpoint. I suppose the active part of us, the observer, can be best described as our conscience. Our conscience can be the spectator of our life movie. The highs and lows that we experience through crisis and grief creates a rollercoaster of emotions. In order to make the most rational and healthy decisions, we must step back from our emotional selves. From this position, we can observe ourselves, and recognize our faults and our true character. We can evaluate ourselves and come to terms with our behavior. For example, we can find out if we are being too critical of ourselves and others, or if we are being unhealthy in our emotions and actions. Once you see yourself as a character in your movie, you can make the necessary changes. Although our conscience is very much a part of us, it is the part of us that we oftentimes ignore, or don't hear at all. When our emotions are overwhelming or powerful, our conscience can be drowned out. Some may call our conscience God, spirit, or some may call it intuition or innate knowledge. Either way, it is there. Our conscience knows best and holds high ethical and moral standards for ourselves and humanity. We can always trust this compass because it operates from a place I can best describe as love. A place of goodness and light.

How do you use your conscience as your spectator? First, you must become aware. Consider your actions and thoughts objectively. Separate *you* from your emotional self. If you need to make a mental picture of yourself, or a drawing in your journal, do it. You can find your own way to do this; there are no rules. Step back and view your personality, thoughts, words, and actions. Reflect on your day, and observe how you reacted in situations, to people, and to yourself. Did you react out of a negative emotion, pain, or fear? Are you too hard on yourself? Begin the practice of non-reaction until you know what is best. Try to recognize your reaction patterns. Take a deep breath before you react to stressful events, and watch yourself play out the scenario. Be aware of patterns of behavior that are a residual effect from negative or hurtful emotions. For example, if your assessment of your emotional self is a pattern of regrets and defeat, you can then realize that is not how you want to represent yourself, and you deserve better. Then you will have a mental example of how you do not want to live, and you can start charting a new course. Do whatever you need to do to be the observer of yourself. This does not need to be an everyday ritual. Just check in with yourself often. It can become an automatic way of living with practice as you become more comfortable listening to your conscience. Challenge yourself to progress towards a higher state of being. Commit yourself to high standards for the betterment of yourself and others. Use your conscience as your compass.

*Be the silent watcher of your thoughts and behavior. You are beneath the thinker. You are the stillness beneath the mental noise. You are the love and joy beneath the pain.*

—ECKHART TOLLE
*The Power of Now: A Guide to Spiritual Enlightenment*

## *Truth #4*

# *Find and absorb inspiration and knowledge*

I searched for inspiration and knowledge almost immediately after my brother passed away. I craved it, I needed it. I had too many questions. I searched for wisdom and understanding, and it helped me tremendously. I first read *Finding Your Way Home* by Melody Beattie.[1] Once I started that book, I needed it every day for positive reinforcement, coaching, healing, love, ideas, and the realization that I was not alone. Others in my family couldn't read until weeks or months after our loss. You must decide what's best for you, but try not to wait too long to dive into some good guidance. You will find that it becomes a crucial tool in regaining your life.

---

[1] Beattie Melody, *Finding Your Way Home: A Soul Survival Kit.*

I found that the right books, quotes, and messages seemed to present themselves in my life as needed. When someone told me to read a certain book, I bought it. When I came across an inspiring quote, I took it to heart and wrote it down. There was always a reason. I never ignored my instinct or intuition about opportunities for guidance and a fresh perspective. A friend of mine gave me a journal right after Kris passed away, and I made it my quote journal. Anytime I came across an inspiring passage or quote I jotted it down. So on any given day I could pick up my journal and find a collection of words that were all meaningful to *me*. Priceless.

## *Challenge:*

As soon as you can, get yourself a journal or a notebook that you dedicate to collecting your favorite quotes. This will be your quote journal. Read inspiring words anywhere you can find them, and write them down. Use these words to give you inspiration and strength. They may be short quotes. They may be long quotes. They may be quotes you've known for years. They may be passages out of books, paragraphs, or maybe even your own words or your mother's, or maybe a Bible verse. Write them down, and visit your quote journal whenever you need. When you feel down, uninspired, unmotivated, upset, or sad, reach for this journal. Read it, and let those inspirational quotes help turn your thoughts around. Words are powerful.

## *Truth #5*

# *You are climbing a mountain*

A loss will automatically place a mountain on your path. A big one. Now that you have a mountain in front of you, what will you do? You must recognize its presence and your ability to climb. More than likely this isn't the first mountain in your life, or maybe it is. But I imagine this is the tallest and steepest of all the mountains you've had to face.

First, sit at the base of that mountain. Allow yourself to hurt, question, and feel. At some point, you need to begin climbing. Climb your mountain. It's in our human nature to be striving, learning, growing, and moving forward in our lives in every way ... spiritually, emotionally, physically, mentally and socially. You cannot allow anything to stand in the way of your growth. Be strong, be a fighter, be a survivor. Your mountain has been set out in front of you. I wouldn't wait too long to begin climbing towards the top. Opportunities await you throughout your climb.

I am happiest when I've strived for and accomplished a goal. The journey is often the true source of happiness. Overcoming little obstacles in the pathway creates momentum. Many people stay stuck, lost, or discontent with their position in their lives and ultimately this causes them to have a low sense of self-worth and a lack of meaning. A loss can certainly keep someone stagnant. I stayed stagnant for four months after the loss of my brother, largely because my living conditions with my husband were emotionally debilitating. You are a different person now because of your loss, and the best thing about it is that you get to choose what kind of person you will be from now on. Choose to fight, choose to win. We must fight for our soul survival, which means climb that mountain!

As you climb, there are milestones to meet. These are points where you can stand on solid ground, look within yourself, and breathe. Take a moment to recognize your progress. You will also realize you have a ways to go, and that's okay. This is a journey. Be patient with yourself, but not so patient that you hold yourself back. Then one day you'll realize the clouds have lifted, the memories are no longer painful, and you are more solid than ever with a clear vision and path. You have a reason to live, and nobody can take that from you. Each moment and step forward and up is a choice.

## Challenge:

On a piece of paper, draw a large mountain. It can simply be two lines that meet at the top. Your pinnacle. Pin your drawing up on a corkboard or somewhere you can view it often. You are climbing this mountain, and you are determined to get to the top. There is no time frame, and you have no idea what's in store. All you know is it will get better each step you take. There are blessings along the way, and you will get to the top. Each time you reach a milestone, whether big or small, write the date and a brief description of the event on the mountain and move a thumbtack (or a marker of some kind) up the side of the mountain to mark your progress. I call every position up the mountain a milestone, even at the very bottom, which is where you are now. Describe at the bottom of the mountain how you feel, and what's going on in your life. For me, the bottom of my mountain read: "Sad, angry, defeated, scared, regretful." I had other milestones that stated, "Went to my first wedding alone in 11 years as a single woman." Another said, "Met a cute guy named Brian." Then a couple months later on another milestone I wrote, "Over Brian, moving on!" And another milestone: "Got through the discovery portion of divorce. Painful."

Imagine how redeeming it will feel to reach the top. This will give you strength. Be your best cheerleader and keep on climbing. Give yourself credit when credit is due. You deserve to acknowledge your progress. Your milestones are your fuel for the journey. Celebrate them, for it is a major accomplishment to reach them, no matter how small they may be. Only you know when you have reached them. A milestone may be reading a new inspiring book, making a new friend, joining a new organization, jogging an extra mile, visiting a gravesite, or just feeling a little bit better than the day before. That is all progress, so mark it as a step up on your mountain.

It's important to realize that as you are climbing, you will also stumble. It's all necessary and a part of your progress, like crossing a rocky river or a fallen tree over the pathway. Consider what Meghan O'Rourke wrote in *The Long Goodbye* about the journey of grief: "It's not an emergence from the cocoon, but a tree growing around an obstruction."[2] Those obstructions and that rocky path will make you stronger. Grow around it, through it, above it. Do not let that steep and narrow path hold you back or make you fearful. Life is a challenge. Nobody said this was going to be easy. It's your life you are fighting for. A good life. This is priceless.

*Mountains are created to be conquered; adversities are designed to be defeated; problems are sent to be solved.*

—WILLIAM ARTHUR WARD

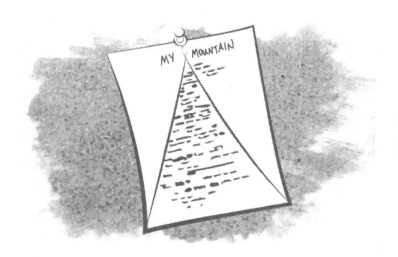

---

[2] O'Rourke Meghan, *The Long Goodbye*

# Truth #6

# *Stay equipped with your soul gear*

The truths in this book are some of your tools and gear to help you climb your mountain to the very top. Always stay equipped with your "soul gear." This means your go-to stash of books, writings, quotes, journals, and items meaningful to you. This can also include intangible items such a comforting image or thought that you can use for inspiration or healing.

I kept my soul gear in my backpack. This backpack is what I would go to when I felt down, depressed, angry, defeated, or lost. I also used my tools on my good days. It contained my inspirational books, my journals, a notepad, and my favorite stones. My soul gear picked me up when I was down. And it validated and encouraged me on my good days. It gave me inspiration, motivation, and so often the right words and message exactly when I needed them.

## Challenge:

Assemble your soul gear bag. It should include your life journal and quote journal, plus any books that are inspiring or helpful to you. Also, you may want to include any meaningful or sentimental items such as a necklace from your grandmother, a rock from the creek bed, a crystal, a note, or a photo. Something that has positive meaning for you. Something inspirational, strong and uplifting. Keep everything in one place, like a tote, folder, box, purse, or a satchel. Something portable. The contents may change as you travel on. Maybe you add to it or omit items as you grow. Maybe you replace books as you finish reading them. But I would suggest that you keep your journals in your bag, as they are important. Keep your soul gear bag as long as you need to. Maybe it's six months, maybe two years, maybe forever. There is no rule. However long you need it to reach the top of your mountain or mountains. And maybe you want to travel with it forever. Up to you.

Part of your soul gear may include certain images or thoughts, a positive visual picture in your mind that is soothing, or a memory of something someone said to you or did for you. During one of my mother's visits, we spent an afternoon painting. We bought small canvases and acrylic and we each made a painting. My mother had never painted on canvas before and was slightly hesitant about her ability. I told her it didn't matter and that it was only for her! "Just paint whatever is in your heart," I said. I figured it would be therapeutic for us to let our minds wander onto canvas for a while.

Her painting blew me away. It was full of meaning. She painted a vision that she turns to from time to time for comfort. She has no idea where the image originated, but it is a place she can go to in her mind to receive peace and joy. Her image shows her and Kris swinging on large swings in the sky, back and forth, jumping off of the swings onto large fluffy clouds, and then bouncing back into the swings. All the while they are smiling and laughing. She painted a happy, dreamy painting of swings hanging from the clouds with a rainbow stretched across the horizon. So now she has a tangible item as part of her soul gear.

Maybe a certain person is part of your soul gear. Let that person know that he or she is important to you in this way, and that there may be times when you need to call him or her, any time of the day or night. Don't hesitate to reach out and call. Tell the truth about your feelings and let this person know how he or she can help you. Many times, you may just need that person to listen, either over the phone, or sitting by your side. Sometimes just the presence of another person is all you need.

You will have many moments of pain. Recognize these moments and reach out for support and inspiration. We are not expected to do this alone. Reach out, open that book, write that thought, read that quote, paint that image, hold that stone, say that prayer, call that friend. It may just save your life.

*Climb the mountains and get their good tidings. Nature's peace will flow into you as sunshine flows into trees. The winds will blow their own freshness into you, and the storms their energy, while cares will drop off like autumn leaves.*

—JOHN MUIR
*Our National Parks*

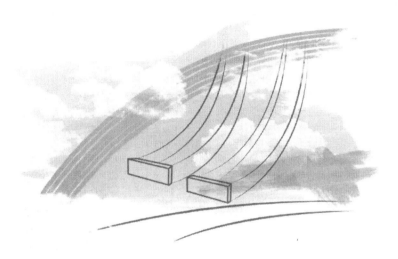

# Truth #7

# *You are not a victim*

Do not view adversities as "bad things" that you don't deserve. Also, do not view yourself as being deserving of your adversities. In other words, don't view yourself as a victim. It is not an issue of deserving or not deserving. Neither of these mindsets is healthy, and both will ultimately keep you in a negative cycle of struggle. You will actually be inviting more problems, because being a victim means you don't have control of your life outcomes. Steve Maraboli says in *Unapologetically You: Reflections on Life and the Human Experience,* "The victim mindset dilutes the human potential. By not accepting personal responsibility for our circumstances, we greatly reduce our power to change them."[3] This is absolutely true.

I understand it may be easy to feel victimized for a while after losing someone, going through a divorce, losing a job,

---

[3] Maraboli Steve, *Unapologetically You: Reflections on Life and the Human Experience*

or receiving the news of an illness, especially if multiple events happen within a short period of time. Small negative incidents—like getting a speeding ticket or spilling a cup of coffee—can add to our feelings of victimization. When things big and small build up, we can feel victimized by God, fate, our peers, or bad luck. This is a dangerous way to live. Unless you change your conscious thoughts and behavior, the "bad luck" will follow you. In the victim mindset, you expect hardships and suffering because you view yourself on the defensive. You see yourself as weaker than your circumstances and believe you deserve them. Negativity attracts and breeds negativity. Change your thinking and perspective, and you will gain control. Gaining emotional and mental control allows freedom from the bondage of victimization.

### *Challenge:*

Challenge yourself to assume responsibility for your circumstances. This doesn't mean you should blame yourself or accept them as is and give up. It means to free yourself from outside people and events controlling your emotions and happiness. It's redeeming, it's self-empowering, and it can change your life. Gracefully accept the roadblocks in front of you as an adventurous challenge that will benefit you in the end. Face your adversities head on with confidence. With this way of thinking, there is absolutely no way for you to lose, no way for you to be defeated, and no way for you to not find blessings from your heart scars. Find your reservoir of strength and courage, and be proud of the fact that you recognize your strength. Be a survivor. It's your choice.

When you feel victimized, overwhelmed by challenges, or uninspired to overcome them, reach for your soul gear bag. Write down your goals, write down the things you have to be grateful for, read something inspiring. Go for a walk, go to the park, visit an old friend or family member. Do something positive. It may not be easy, but just do it. Take control of your actions and reactions and choose to overcome. Pull yourself out of that funk. It's tough to think clearly while in a negative mindset. You need to know your action plan when times get tough because tough times are bound to happen.

*Every test in our life makes us bitter or better, every problem comes to break us or make us. The choice is ours whether we become victim or victor.*

—Unknown

## <u>*Truth #8*</u>

# *God never leaves you—*
# *God does not punish you*

The common theme for those who live a spiritual life is that God is always present. Maybe you don't believe in God; maybe you have a hard time believing in anything. That is okay. I'm not here to preach or try to persuade you of God's existence. I can only tell of my own experience as best I can. For me, God is something that is not describable. God is something I feel and something that I know has guided and protected me throughout my journey. I understand that for some, it's hard to believe in something you can't prove, see, or tangibly experience. Or you may have an even stronger faith in an organized religion. Whatever your beliefs are, this may be the time to dig in and experience it more than you ever have before. Maybe differently than before. Explore different thoughts or philosophies if you feel inclined to. Let it evolve if you feel it needs to. Develop it, and hold tight to it.

Regardless of the specifics of your belief, there's always the option of having faith. A positive outlook, a hopeful perspective, faith in a brighter future. Or perhaps believing in God is a collection of your own thoughts, feelings, images, and actions that makes sense to *you*. In her book *Tiny Beautiful Things*, Cheryl Strayed responds to a woman whose baby was in the hospital with a brain tumor. This mother was questioning the existence of God, as it was uncertain if the baby was going to live. Strayed didn't claim to have any answers, but in part of her response she wrote, "What if you allowed your God to exist in the simple words of compassion others offer to you?"[4] Even the most simple words or experiences we encounter can be perceived as incredibly meaningful. It can be acknowledged as God if you so choose.

Have you ever tried to recognize and embrace your daily miracles? Small and large, I believe we are in the presence of miracles all the time. We don't always have to understand the *why* and the *how* in order to appreciate them. We don't even have to have a specific spiritual or religious belief. Maybe your faith resides in the existence of love and compassion of and for people, or the emergence of the sun in the eastern sky in the morning hours. Believe in these miracles. And it's okay to call it God. I do. Whatever your belief, find security and peace in it throughout your loss and after. God is within us, God is outside of us, and God surrounds us. God is always present and available, if you choose to believe.

It may be easy to wonder why, if God is so great and loving, God would allow us to feel this much pain, or

---

[4] Strayed Cheryl, *Tiny Beautiful Things*

"take" someone away from us. I do not believe anything is ever taken from us, without the potential of at least an equal value in return. It is true that nothing will replace the loss of a loved one. Nothing will completely fill the void left by their physical absence. But the experience of any kind of loss itself has the capability to offer a new perspective on life, new opportunities for change and growth, and deep understanding. Realize that nobody, especially God, is out to get you or punish you. We are all granted blessings if we choose to take the path of understanding. Take one day at a time with an open heart and mind, and trust that answers will come when they are supposed to.

## *Challenge:*

When I want to connect with God, I need to remove the mind chatter that tells me I am lost or disconnected. There is always a connection to be had with God. It is up to us to feel the connection. God wants us to be happy, free, and passionate. From time to time, we will all falter and feel God-less, or life-less. Life will feel disrupted and without meaning. We'll have our days of questioning and confusion. We will feel angry towards God. We will feel lost. But as we rise above our hardships and seek understanding, we will find wisdom.

In my most challenging days after losing my brother and husband, I put up hand-written messages on small and large pieces of paper around my house. I taped one quote by Napoleon Hill on my bathroom mirror: "Whatever the mind can conceive and believe, the mind can achieve." In my living room I put up the following: "Do not be afraid, for I am with you," "Surrender fully to the experience and trust," "Don't take anything personal," and "Love is the answer." The positivity cultivated and strengthened my connection to a higher power. I felt safe. I had to see these quotes every day around my house, and I believed them when I read them. I needed a visual reminder of my faith in better days ahead.

Try this: put up positive notes in your environment that help cultivate a sense of faith, a way to feel protected and safe. The notes can be on sticky notes, notebook paper, or even big pieces of construction paper. They can be simply stated or colorful with design. Secondly, you must believe what you read, and feel what you believe. Just know that what you feel is *real*. That is the ultimate trust in faith. No questions. Believe in the miracles of your daily life. The miracle of waking in the morning with the opportunity for another day. The miracle of forgiveness and strength. The miracle of your faith. The miracle that God is always there. We are not being punished, so rid your mind of that philosophy. God believes in us and our abilities not only to cope but also to thrive. Don't settle for mediocrity, pain patterns, or defeat.

Dive into your faith. Explore a higher power. Connect with the goodness of God. You need to feel comforted, supported and guided through your grief. In fact, we need this at all times. With faith and awareness, we can rise above any circumstance.

*The light of God surrounds me; the love of God enfolds me; the power of God protects me; the presence of God watches over me. Wherever I am, God is.*

—JAMES DILLET FREEMAN

# Truth #9

# *Be like water*

Throughout my grieving, I developed a feeling of internal guidance that I would picture as water, like a river running through me. This guidance gave me peace and hope for the moment, hope for my week, and hope for my future. I had to believe in something, and that *something* was deep within. Nobody could offer it to me; nothing anyone could say would make me feel it. I had to recognize it, and I had to claim it as my own. It is a gift, and everyone has it available to him or her.

This doesn't mean you should stop doing, stop trying, stop striving, or stop growing. What you should do is let down your guard and release all fear. This will allow you to breathe, to accept what you cannot change or control, and to rely on what you *can* control. Find your undercurrent river of faith. It is there. Be still to find it and then flow like water through your experiences. You have to surrender to the process for a little while. Again, this doesn't mean give up. It just means you can stop trying to force changes on things or people that cannot be changed. What you can do is shift your perspective, meaning, or position according to the circumstances. If you want to be a survivor and find meaning within the pain, you must not allow yourself to accept roadblocks as if you are a victim.

Watch a river or the water at the edge of the ocean and notice how it always finds its way through, around, and over its surroundings. At times it fights its way through small openings or shifts abruptly. At other times it is peaceful and serene, completely content with its position. No matter what obstacles are in its path, it always keeps its properties. Isn't this how we should also attempt to live? There is a time to fight for our survival, a time to gently go with the flow, and most importantly a time to find peace within our environment and selves.

Our losses create the necessity to fight. Not in a way that is harmful or violent, but in a way that is passionate and has a positive driving force behind it. Fight for your right to live happily and to be the best that you can possibly be. There will always be sharp rocks and unexpected barriers in our paths to work our way through and around, but these obstacles are what help us grow, and give us opportunities to expand our minds.

## Challenge:

Picture in your mind a river, a peaceful stream, or creek—a flowing stream of water, gracefully moving over and through rocks, always knowing its destination with no hesitation. Now picture this river within you. Behind the water is an unseen guidance. Just as there is an unseen guidance in your life journey. It gives you wisdom, it gives you strength. Trust in the process of your life. Be open to the possibilities that lie ahead of you, with no assumptions, no inhibitions, no fear.

*Always be like water. Float in the times of pain or dance like waves along the wind which touches its surface.*

—SANTOSH KALWAR

.

## *Truth #10*

# *You are your friend— love and trust yourself*

Your loss may make you feel like you can't trust anyone or anything. But you can always trust yourself. Believe in your strength and your inner wisdom. You must take this opportunity and pull from the reserves of your own strength. True friends will be there for you and are very important, but honestly you only have yourself to count on for the long haul. You need to nurture your own spirit through your own thoughts and words. You are stronger than you know. I'm convinced that we each have a reservoir of strength deep down inside us, but finding it takes a whole lot of determination, endurance, and trust. Find silence and listen to yourself. Trust what you hear, trust what you feel, and trust your instincts. View yourself as a friend, someone you truly love and take care of. Tell yourself you care about you, love you, and will be patient with you through this process. Your body needs to hear this. Your spirit needs to hear this.

Your thoughts are one of the single most important things for your health and well-being. The emotional stress that comes along with grief can be taxing on your body physically, so try to remember to speak kindly to yourself, and your physical body will listen and react positively, as well. As hurtful emotions come up, tell yourself it's okay, and replace the hurt with love. Recognize that what you're going through is not easy. Going through a major loss is one of the most difficult things you will ever have to face, so be patient with yourself.

## *Challenge:*

Throughout your days, practice loving yourself. One way to do this is to create or find a quote, a mantra, a saying of some kind that you can remember and repeat to yourself daily. It might feel awkward, but talk to your body. Talk to your spirit. You could say, *The cells in my body are happy. The cells in my body are healthy.* Another simple reminder you could say is, *Every day, in every way, I am better and better.* I repeat words such as these as often as I can. As you say it, it's important to feel it and visualize it. Believe it to be true, and it will be. Write down your mantra and repeat it in your head often, with conviction. Put your positive quote on your work desk, in your car, or by your nightstand.

Shortly after my separation, and during my transition from living with my husband to living alone, I wrote out an affirmation that I laminated and posted on my nightstand. When I awoke each morning, it was there, and I read it aloud before I got out of bed.

*Today is my day! I am grateful for another opportunity to move forward with my passions and goals. It is up to me how I spend my time and energy. I choose to be joyful and enthusiastic. I choose to be positive and see any obstacles as opportunities to grow and learn. I choose to love others, treat others with respect and fulfill my duties for the highest good of the world. I am resilient, strong, smart, healthy and happy. I trust my instincts, and believe I am guided by God each and every day, in each and every way.*

Give yourself a mental and emotional hug every day. Wrap loving thoughts around your heart. Every cell in your body will feel this and appreciate it more than you know.

*You, yourself, as much as anybody in the entire universe, deserve your love and affection.*

—BUDDHA

## *Truth #11*

# *Connect with nature*

Nature has a way of encouraging a safe and meaningful feeling in us. In nature, a perfectly harmonious exchange is displayed between all living creatures at all times. To me, there is no stronger example of God than nature, and whether or not you view God in the same manner as me, nature can have a very positive impact on your life. It will offer to you whatever you want and more. There's an undeniable energy in nature, which can be brought within ourselves if we allow it.

### *Challenge:*

Find a time of day or night when you are best able to connect to nature. Go outdoors. Find a local botanical garden, a lake, the beach, a park, a field, the woods, hiking trails, or a nature center. Maybe it's your own back yard. The main objective is to be in nature, amongst the trees, grass, and flowers. Go there and listen, feel, surrender. Just exist in that moment and breathe. Know that you are connected to all that is good. Develop an appreciation for and a fascination of nature. Have you really looked at the details of a wildflower? Have you really appreciated the growth of a tree, realizing that the roots grow deeper than the tree is tall? Have you ever watched a blue jay as it gathers its nesting supplies, knowing exactly what it should be doing with no hesitation? Having a childlike curiosity toward nature and wildlife can be healing. Be mesmerized. Allow the intricate details, complex design, fragrant smells, and the boisterous color palate of nature to intrigue you. It's free. Enjoy it and learn from the experience it offers you.

*Those who contemplate the beauty of the earth find reserves of strength that will endure as long as life lasts.*

—RACHEL CARSON
*The Sense of Wonder*

# *Truth #12*

# *We always have a choice*

Every day we have choices in what we do, what we say, whom we surround ourselves with, what we eat, what we think, how we react, and what we pursue. For the most part, we are in complete control of our lives. If you feel off course, it's your choice to find a different path. As you are climbing your mountain, you will have moments of clarity, and you will know if you're on the right path or not. It will just feel *right*. When I had these moments, I pictured myself on a little flat plateau of the mountain, where all was calm, safe and comfortable, and I could enjoy the vista from a place of security, knowing I was on the right path to a fulfilling goal. These moments of clarity were my milestones—assurance that I was on the right track.

Reflect, assess where you are, where you've come from, how you feel, and how long you've felt that way. Don't form emotional habits that keep you stagnant, stuck, or backed into a corner. Also, for any positive growth, we need to recognize any behavioral or emotional patterns that we may have. Most everyone has them. These could be patterns or habits you were raised with or ones you have acquired through your life. They may be patterns that you are noticing due to your loss. Do you tend to get jealous easily, are you self-deprecating, are you judgmental, are you defensive, are you a pushover, are you fearful of change? Other examples of emotional habits are: feeling sorry for yourself when something goes wrong (victimization), feeling like you aren't worthy of anything better, or feeling lonely because you are not confident enough to face the world or new situations. The goal is to become free of blockages and emotional baggage and recognize your options for change. It won't happen overnight, and we cannot put a time frame on it. Awareness will keep you from getting stuck in emotional habits. As you view yourself from an outsider's perspective as discussed in Truth #3, *Be aware of your emotions*, you'll see how you react in situations, and your emotions that arise. Are there any consistent themes or reoccurring reactions that are producing negative or unsatisfying results? Once you are aware of your patterns, you suddenly have the power to change them, and in return change your experience.

## *Challenge:*

Every day, practice being in control of your actions, thoughts, and words. Yes, it's easier said than done, but with practice it will become the most positive habit you've ever developed. When someone says or does something distasteful to you, tell yourself to be wiser than your initial negative reaction. Take a moment and decide whether or not it's worth it to let that person or situation get the best of you. Protect yourself from damaging thought behavior, and in return you will protect your physical and spiritual self too.

You may need some time to gain control of repeated anger, jealousy, or feelings of victimization. These emotions and thoughts are normal, but it's important to realize that when they become habitual, they create blockages in our lives. Once we take control of our reactions and emotions, we open up a new energetic field for positive returns. With practice, you will eventually feel empowered and relieved to have control over your life and to your reactions to situations that are realistically out of your control. I promise you will feel empowered, and your stress level will diminish considerably. Be the master of your destiny. This is your gift.

*True power, true spiritual power—the kind that warriors are made of—is not based on bitterness, resentments, and hatred. Power comes from a base of being clear, knowing who we are, and feeling a quiet confidence that we can speak our truth. We face our enemies and calmly yet forcefully identify the dangers, the manipulations, the betrayals, then we reverse the negative energy so we can protect and defend ourselves.*

—MELODY BEATTIE
*Finding Your Way Home: A Soul Survival Kit*

*It is not in the stars to hold our destiny, but in ourselves.*

—WILLIAM SHAKESPEARE

# *Truth #13*

# *We all have a purpose*

Knowing what our life purpose is can be challenging. Trusting the process may be the most important part of being led to your bliss. After a loss, you may end up realizing that what you once found important or a driving factor in your life no longer is. A completely different calling may surface, and you may realize it is what you were always looking for anyway. A loss can also make you lose interest in life, in your career, in everything. Grief can make you feel unproductive, unsettled, depressed, and without passion. It can make you think, *What's the point?* This is common and normal for the first few months after an impactful loss. My losses made me question my inner purpose. I realized that the career I was working in was in reality my husband's career and passion. I didn't listen to myself and pursue my heart's endeavors. But my losses forced me to take a hard look at what was going to make me happy. It was as if grief had torn apart the puzzle, and piece by piece I started putting me back together. Only now, the pieces all fit properly together and created the intended picture. I found a burning desire to find my passion. I wanted to feel alive with purpose and reason every morning when I woke.

It can be difficult to determine what our calling is, especially if we are tangled up in an unhealthy way of life, an unhealthy relationship with someone, or an unhealthy relationship with ourselves. Sometimes a tragedy may force us out of our numbness and content discontentment. Trust the subtle nudges that encourage you to press forward, even if it's in a direction you don't understand. Be okay with stepping outside of your comfort zone. Take the first step. Don't be afraid. You will only regret what you do not try. Your intuition will guide you if you let it.

## *Challenge:*

In your life journal, write down everything you've been interested in throughout your life. As a child, as an adolescent, as an adult. Any time. Write down all the subtle or not so subtle ideas you've had for your life passions, career, or hobbies. Write down what makes you happy, what makes you lose track of time. What activities allow you to be the best version of yourself? What is it that makes you tick? What fulfills you? Write down activities you enjoy, items you enjoy, no matter how vague or detailed. Maybe it's animals, nature, numbers, helping others, painting, building, traveling, cooking, selling, or creating. If you are 100 percent happy with your position now, maybe there's no need to do this exercise. Or maybe you have other passions or hobbies you would like to pursue alongside your career or lifestyle. You must think, *when I'm 80 years old, what will I wish I had accomplished? Will I have regrets?* What continues to sit at the back of your mind? Put it on paper. Maybe your first journal entry is just scribbles about what you love and want to do in your life, and maybe after more thought over the course of a month, or two, or three, you begin putting your passions into complete sentences and goals.

As you move forward with your journaling and have a more solid idea of your life interests, write your interests down as direct actions, such as the following: "I will write a book," or "I will start my own baked goods company," or "I will take a photography class in the next three months," or "I will build a dining room table," or "I will begin volunteering time at the homeless shelter one day a week." Date your journal entries. Now, go back and read your passion entries often, but the most important thing is to watch your days unfold. Be aware of who you meet along the way. Pay attention to those people who just *seem special and meant to be in your life.* The universe has a way of putting people and situations into your life strategically to either motivate you, encourage you, inspire you, or be a vehicle for your growth. Hints may be subtle, but they are there. Do not take any day, moment, or person for granted. You can learn something in every situation that is presented to you. You must be out doing positive things, though. Be aware of opportunity and take action. If you are sitting at home all day long watching soap operas, trust me, the universe is not going to work with you in your favor. You must be out following your heart, treating others fairly, loving others, loving yourself, and being aware. Even if you aren't exactly sure what your passions are, you can make tiny steps every day to move in the right direction. Ask for guidance and say, *I do not know at this time what I need to do for passion in my life, so please guide me, motivate me, and help me to be aware when opportunities present themselves so I can find my bliss.* Trust your instinct, and follow through with the small gestures that can advance you, including opportunities placed in your path. Be proactive when you have the urge to move forward with something, talk to someone, or take a risk. If you have a choice to go to that social event, wedding, lecture, do it. You'll be amazed at whom you'll meet and what you'll learn. One day you'll understand why you were led to go.

*Your purpose in life is to find your purpose and give your whole heart and soul to it.*

—GAUTAMA BUDDHA

*If one advances confidently in the direction of his dreams, and endeavors to live the life which he has imagined, he will meet with a success unexpected in common hours.*

—HENRY DAVID THOREAU
*Walden*

# Truth #14

# *The past and the future do not exist*

This seems like a logical thought, and it is. Yet most humans do not operate as if it is so. It's very common to remain stuck in the past and feel anxious about the future. But this is not a healthy approach to living. Instead, take responsibility for your words and actions, learn from your experience, but do not dwell on any kind of negative thoughts about the past. In fact, don't dwell on thoughts about the past at all, unless you are attempting to learn lessons. I will speak of this again in a later truth, but deep forgiveness of the past will also allow us to move on and live more presently. Nothing can reverse what is done. All we can do is change our patterns and emotional habits. Just the same, there's no need to be in a constant state of anxiousness about the future. Make the necessary plans and steps of action to advance, but also find moments to really connect with your current environment, right now.

Do your best *now*, feel your life *now*. Exist in the current moment. Of course we always need to plan and compare options. But if we are consistently neglecting now, and always looking into the future for contentment and answers, we are not living fully. Anticipating the future can really be a form of fear. This can be one of the most challenging of all the truths because we are conditioned to retain memories and plan for the future. Yes, there are many important memories to hold on to and cherish, but when memories feel unsettling, regretful or painful, we need to seek resolution. We also tend to hold grudges against others and ourselves, which again is a total waste of mind space and energy. You are only holding yourself back when you hold a grudge. Resentments and regrets are only memories that cloud our reality and hinder our opportunity for freedom and happiness.

## *Challenge:*

What if we accepted, forgave, and learned from our past? And what if we had faith in our future, all while living in the present? Doesn't that make sense? Be conscious of your thoughts and what you hyper-focus on, and begin bringing your attention to your present moment. You will fall back to your old habits from time to time, but with practice, it will get easier. We are not perfect, and you may never reach a point of perfect union with now. That is normal. But with conscious effort, I believe we can find a fairly consistent state of "now awareness."

One way to find "now awareness" is by sitting in nature, or any quiet and comfortable space. This could be at a park, your living room, or your back yard. Be present with your surroundings. Listen, watch, become one with the experience. Connect with your physical body and let go of all fears and concerns. Do not let yourself focus on an emotion, problem, or situation. Consciously let it all drift away. Release from your mind what no longer serves you in a positive manner. Mentally send it away from your being. Give your mind a clean slate with no demanding thoughts. Accept the past as non-existent and merely a memory that can be forgiven. Accept your higher power to be the guide for your future. This leaves it unnecessary to worry, as the past and future are taken care of. Connect with *right now*. Right now is when we feel joy. Right now is when we feel acceptance. Right now is when we feel breath flowing in and out of our bodies. Right now is when we feel alive. Take a deep breath and bring your mind to the present moment. Relax your shoulders, unclench your jaw, and close your eyes for a moment. Draw your awareness to now and realize this is all you have. This moment. This sacred moment.

Now that you know what being present feels like, you can practice staying present throughout your regular daily schedule. And when you need a reminder of what being present feels like, take yourself back to this comfortable space. Take time throughout your day to recognize your presence in this world. Experience what now truly feels like. Nobody else can do it for you. You are the gatekeeper. Live in presence with no fear. Tell yourself all is well and all will continue to be well. You are safe in this moment. Like Eckhart Tolle said in his book, *The Power of Now*, if a tree or eagle is asked what time it is, it would say, "Well, of course, it's now. The time is now. What else is there?"[5]

*Your outer journey may contain a million steps; your inner journey only has one: the step you are taking right now.*

—ECKHART TOLLE
*The Power of Now: A Guide to Spiritual Enlightenment*

---

[5] Tolle Eckhart, *The Power of Now: A Guide to Spiritual Enlightenment*

# *Truth #15*

# *Write your heart out*

If you know how to write, you are a writer! This is another reminder from a previous challenge to visit your journal. Or maybe you want to keep a different collection of writings in another notebook or file. We all have thoughts, feelings, and something to say. So why not write them down? It is therapeutic and healing, even if you don't realize it. Let your mind drift; translate emotions onto paper or onto your computer. Your words may jump around from idea to idea, thought to thought, and story to story, and that is perfectly okay. It's for you, not anyone else. Nobody's grading your journal or your thoughts. This is your mind, your life, your story. You will feel better after writing down your thoughts, and one day you'll look back on your pages and realize how far you've come.

For me, my writing became a safe haven. It was a way for me to express myself as if I were talking to a friend. In the beginning, I wrote letters to Kris. His 30th birthday, Christmas, my birthday. Other times I wrote about how I was doing. How I was feeling. What happened that day, the good and bad. As I progressed, I began to notice that I would naturally find purpose and understanding through my writing. At times I began an entry saying that life hurt, I was sad, and I was scared, but by the end of the entry my attitude would shift to positivity, faith, and gratitude. Journaling taps into the subconscious and allows for deep insights to come forth. With a clear perspective, I was often able to come up with an action plan or resolution. This allowed me to lay my head down at night with peace.

## *Challenge:*

Get out that life journal and write. Maybe you want to write about your daily experiences and feelings. Maybe you want to write poetry or a song. Maybe you want to write your story. Maybe you want to write a letter to your loved one who has passed. Whatever your heart tells you to write that day, write it. It's not about composition or order. It's not about grammar or trying to please anyone. It's for you, and only you.

*Be yourself. Above all, let who you are, what you are, what you believe shine through every sentence you write, every piece you finish.*

—JOHN JAKES

*Truth #16*

# Embrace solitude and independence

In the initial days of grief, you should surround yourself with those you love and who love you. This is an important part of the healing process for humans. Gather with those who comfort you. You need to lean on those people you trust and who can listen and attempt to understand. This support will help hold you up, and also help get you back on your feet. Then at some point you need to begin stepping out into the world again—alone. It's important to discover what your life feels like within a bit of solitude. Just as comfortable as you are with people, you should strive for that same comfort in being alone.

Being alone can be tough, and even more so when you are experiencing a loss. It can be uncomfortable to face our thoughts and feelings in times of hardship and turmoil. We can feel isolated or stuck in our own heads, so we may crave the presence of others just to avoid our own minds. The distraction of another person's presence can give the illusion of helping us through a day, or a moment. A friend or a social setting can be extremely comforting and healing and will always be a necessary part of your life, but learning to be alone can be one of the most amazing and beneficial lessons of all. If we can learn to feel full contentment and joy in solitude, we can begin to claim ourselves to be whole. Learning how to sleep alone, wake up alone, make breakfast alone, shop alone, hike alone, take road trips alone, and think—just thinking, sitting still, all alone, can be an invaluable and sacred journey. I'm not saying you should become a hermit and close yourself off from social life and friends. This will lead to an unhealthy lifestyle which lends itself to loneliness. Solitude does not need to feel lonely. In fact, solitude should not feel lonely. You should seek balance and learn to be at peace with solitude, all while maintaining healthy relationships with friends and family. We need both the social aspect of life and the serenity of solitude.

If you have gone through a divorce, getting to know yourself again as a single individual is empowering. Take the time to explore who you are and who you want to be. Invest in your growth and individuality. You owe it to yourself, and you owe it to any relationship you might enter into in the future. You will be a better version of yourself if you do this, and you'll have more fulfilling relationships as a result.

## *Challenge:*

You will only be content with solitude if you love yourself. In keeping with Truth #10, *You are your friend—love and trust yourself,* you must learn to view yourself as a friend, someone you take care of. Encouraging yourself to embrace solitude will help you do this, and loving yourself will help you embrace solitude. They work hand in hand. Recognize your fears of being alone, and challenge yourself to face those fears. One small step at a time, step outside of your comfort zone into the wilderness of yourself. The darkness, the light, and all of the unknown territories of your spirit. Encourage it all to surface. You must live in faith, a faith stronger than your fears. As you embark on this journey of soul-searching solitude, you will regain more than you imagined. I dove in and faced my weaknesses, my fears, and all the parts that I wanted to deny, but deep down knew I shouldn't. In my moments of solitude, I recognized my strengths and weaknesses and realized how to better myself. Reflecting on my habits, patterns, and the moments where I went wrong brought peace and resolution. For example, in my moments of reflection, I accepted that I wasn't always the best wife I could have been or the wife I know I want to be. I know I failed time and time again. I've failed a lot. But more importantly, I learned that failures do not define us; they help create a better version of us. The way we react to and grow from our failures and adversities defines who we are.

Write down your fears about being alone. Express what you fear about yourself, and why you might avoid solitude. Write down incidences of when you have avoided being alone, and write down what you could have done differently. Next, write down some specific actions you can take to be alone, to begin detaching from any distractions, whether it be people or cell phones. Are there a couple of hours this week or next when you can commit to having no distractions and just being with yourself? Plan it and do it. During this time, honestly reflect on yourself with no harsh judgments, with only the intention of understanding, growth, and wisdom. Remember to love yourself. This is most important.

*Loneliness is the poverty of self; solitude is the richness of self.*

—MAY SARTON
*Journal of a Solitude*

## *Truth #17*

# *Be grateful*

I believe that gratitude is one of the most healing emotions a person can experience. Sure, we often say we're thankful, or nonchalantly express thanks, but I'm talking about deep, sincere, authentic thankfulness for things seen and unseen. There's always something to be grateful for. Life itself is reason enough to be thankful. Deep, honest gratefulness opens doors to God, freedom, opportunity, and the true you. Something magical happens when we truly express an honest and humble feeling of gratitude. It is an experience. A spiritual experience. It is a balloon once tethered to a string, but now afloat in the sky, free from the human tendency to complain about victimization, circumstance, or emotional bondage. Gratitude is powerful.

You may not have everything you want, but you just may have everything you need. For now, anyway. When you consider what others who are less fortunate are dealing with and don't have, it's easy to realize your blessings. This deep gratitude makes us humble. It grounds us and allows us to feel wrapped in love. It radiates from the core of our heart, and others can feel it. It opens us up to recognize the blessings and the love we know we have received and the love and blessings we can pass on to others. This energy is never-ending. Keep the cycle going and give back what you have received.

In my darkest days and brightest days, I lay in my bed at night and express my gratitude. With this grateful mindset, absolutely nothing can destroy me, hurt me, or take away my blessings. And the same goes for you. As deeply as I had hurt, my gratitude was always deeper. I was not a victim; I was gaining strength. I was thankful for the hard times. I was thankful for the tears I'd cried. I was thankful for the loneliness. I was thankful for my divorce. I was thankful for the lessons Kris was teaching me through his life on earth and also through his death. I was thankful for the new friends I was acquiring. I was thankful for the roof over my head, the warm bed I slept in, the food I had when I awoke, my family's support, my ability to recognize the benefits of adversity, God's love and protection, and my future. I would frequently speak aloud what I was thankful for, and I would sleep through the night in peace, knowing there was a new day ahead—another step up my mountain.

## Challenge:

Create a gratitude box. Dedicate a vessel of some kind to contain what you are grateful for. On small pieces of paper, write down things, experiences, and people you are thankful for, and drop them into this vessel. Maybe your vessel has sentimental value, like your grandmother's jewelry box or your father's old cigar box. Maybe it's a mason jar. Maybe it's just a shoebox. I used a wooden trinket box my brother had made for me one year in his high school shop class.

When I first created my gratitude box, in it I had a piece of paper for each of my immediate family members, my house, my job, my health, my dog, my cat, my wisdom, my strength, and my adversities. I became thankful for the hardships I had to go through because I knew I was learning lessons that I could not have learned otherwise. You should attempt to do the same. If you want, draw a simple picture along with the words or the name of the person. Make the notes as pretty or as simple as you like. Put the papers in the box and label the box "Gratitude Box." Every day, or once a week—however often you want—pull out a piece of paper and remind yourself of how blessed you are to have that person, thing, or experience in your life. Keep your gratitude box accessible. Keep adding to it as the days pass. Before you know it, your vessel will be full.

Also, before you fall asleep at night, think of all the things you are thankful for. Visualize all of them one by one, and *feel* how grateful you are for those things, events, and people. Give thanks for the house you live in, the bed you sleep in, your family and friends, your pets, your job, your safety, your wisdom, the day you just experienced, your tomorrow, your guidance, your life! Also be thankful for your adversities, because they allow you the opportunity to grow, learn, and become a better person. Even if you don't understand why you are going through these trials, be grateful for the faith that you have in a higher power to show you the way and help you heal. Be grateful for the void you are in and the unknown. Be thankful for the good things that are sure to come.

*Gratitude unlocks the fullness of life. It turns what we have into enough, and more. It turns denial into acceptance, chaos to order, confusion to clarity. It can turn a meal into a feast, a house into a home, a stranger into a friend.*

—MELODY BEATTIE
*Finding Your Way Home: A Soul Survival Kit.*

*To speak gratitude is courteous and pleasant, to enact gratitude is generous and noble, but to live gratitude is to touch Heaven.*

—JOHANNES A. GAERTNER

## *Truth #18*

# *Each and every day matters*

Sounds overly simple, but it's also very true. We shouldn't take one day for granted, as life is a gift. As mentioned in Truth #14, *The past and the future do not exist.* We need to appreciate our present moment. Be presently active in your daily life, whether you are reading a book, talking to a friend, doing manual labor, playing, working, praying, or participating in any daily activity. We can only fully appreciate and absorb the goodness of our days if we are fully present in what we are doing. Our daily decisions, actions, and thoughts form our lives as a whole. Consider every day a gift, an opportunity. Paint your painting, sculpt your sculpture, create your reality. Intend on doing your best and giving your best. When you do this, the best will come back to you.

### *Challenge:*

There is no act too small or insignificant. Practice positive thinking and positive acting. While embracing the *now*, do something each day to better yourself or better others, and in return for both, you will better your mind and life. On sad days, offer yourself positive affirmations, go for a hike, or write down a list of all the things you love and appreciate about yourself. Pick yourself a wildflower. On your better days, offer something to someone else. A compliment. A hug. A handwritten note of appreciation. A favor. A wildflower.

The positive efforts of our thoughts and actions towards ourselves and others is the thread that helps weave the pattern of our lives. Our days are the opportunity. We have been given the ability to think, choose, and act through free will. It is up to us how we respond, how we act, how we think, and how we choose to treat others. Since we have this capability, each day matters. Each day matters a lot. Act upon it wisely.

*Always hold fast to the present. Every situation, indeed every moment, is of infinite value, for it is the representative of a whole eternity.*

—JOHANN WOLFGANG VON GOETHE

## *Truth #19*

# *Take care of your body*

A body going through grief is a body going through intense stress, so start taking care of your body now. Do not wait till you start noticing symptoms. Stress can be defined as the brain's response to any demand. Sometimes stress is necessary, mild, or harmless, such as the stress needed for quick decision making, commuting to work, or running a race. Other times, stress is more extreme, like when you experience a divorce, lose a loved one, or move through a major life change. Nerve chemicals and hormones are released during times of stress. According to the National Institute of Mental Health, when stress becomes chronic, and the body's reaction isn't for immediate survival, your digestive, excretory, and reproductive systems stop working normally. If the stress response lasts too long, these symptoms can lead to more severe health problems such as high blood pressure, depression, anxiety, and heart disease. Not everyone's physical body will experience stress the same way. Some may experience issues with their digestive systems, while others may experience sleeplessness, mood swings, skin issues, irritability, or headaches. With a suppressed immune system, those going through chronic stress are prone to more frequent and severe viral infections, such as the common cold or flu.[6]

In my case, my hair got thinner, my face broke out for months, and my fingernails became paper thin and peeled like crazy. Not the most pleasant things to experience on top of grief. Fortunately, research shows that lifestyle changes and stress-relieving techniques are beneficial and can minimize the effects of stress on the body. Taking practical steps to maintain your health and outlook can reduce or prevent these effects.[7] Be on top of the game, and start supporting your system now. Take supportive supplements to help your body while it works overtime. Due to the emotional stress, you may need to increase your vitamins and minerals. Also, eat a healthy diet full of fresh, non-processed foods. Be aware of your sugar, caffeine, and alcohol intake. Get out and walk, run, hike, play sports, whatever it is you enjoy. You may not feel like getting out and being active, but your body will thank you once you do. You need to get the blood flowing and your heart rate up. This will all, in turn, make you feel better mentally. Your body produces feel-good endorphins as you engage in physical activity. These endorphins are a type of neurotransmitter in the brain that helps in treating mild forms of depression and anxiety. In addition, eating a healthy diet and enhancing

---

[6] National Institute of Mental Health
[7] National Institute of Mental Health

both the amount and quality of your sleep may be beneficial."[8]

## *Challenge:*

Throughout my days of chronic stress, I stayed active through running, walking, and pushing myself into new exercise territory, such as Zumba. I had never done it before, and it was very healing for me. For one whole hour, my ex, my divorce, my attorney, my struggles, and stress did not exist. All that existed was what I was doing in that moment, listening to the music, following the instructor, dancing. I smiled. I laughed. I felt alive. This experience of joy became part of my enduring journey towards happiness. I walked out of that class with more energy, improved confidence, and a smile on my face.

I challenge you to stay active. Go for a 30-minute walk, swim a few laps in the pool, log some time on the treadmill, or get on the mat in a yoga class. And change it up. Keep it interesting so you don't get bored with it. Step outside of your comfort zone and do something you have never done before. Sign up for a new class at the YMCA, join an outdoor adventure club, start bike riding or horseback riding, or simply start walking or hiking on new trails. Take new routes, experience new places, and see new faces. Do not be afraid. And remember, it's okay to laugh at yourself! A smile is a smile.

Fueling your body is just as important as getting exercise. With your system working overtime during stress, you owe it to yourself to properly maintain healthy eating habits. Eat fresh fruits and vegetables often, limit your sugar and processed foods, limit your

---

[8] American Psychological Association, *Understanding Chronic Stress*

caffeine intake, limit or eliminate fast foods, and support your system with multi-vitamins and minerals. Ask your health care professional for some natural supplements you can take to support you through the stress. Our food is our fuel. The better quality the fuel, the better the output. The better the strength. The better the endurance. The better the resilience. The better the life.

*Taking care of your mental and physical health is just as important as any career move or responsibility.*

—MIREILLE GUILIANO

## *Truth #20*

# *Get good sleep*

Sleep: it's that one thing that we all know we need but find hard to get—especially in stressful times. Getting good sleep improves memory, spurs creativity, helps maintain a healthy weight, lowers stress, decreases anxiety, helps with emotional stability, improves immune function, and benefits overall health and well-being.

I know some of my family members had a very hard time going to sleep and staying asleep after Kris passed away. This is understandable considering the pain and restlessness that a loss inflicts on us. Our minds tend to run recklessly sometimes, and when the mind is on full speed, we are unable to rest. This is acceptable for a while, but eventually you need to find a solution to the insomnia. Your body and mind need it more than ever now. How do you view sleep? How do you view night time? In my mind, sleep has always been my friend. I desire my eight hours of sleep because it allows me to connect with my subconscious; it allows a little happy vacation.

On the other hand, some people may get too much sleep. Sleep can be used as a getaway. There's a difference between desiring and appreciating sleep and desiring a constant escape through sleep—an escape from reality, which can become habit-forming. Thinking about sleep as a way out of reality is more than likely a sign of depression. Depression can also do the opposite and hinder you from sleeping. Either way, if you are feeling chronically depressed beyond the one-year mark of your loss, you need to seek help from professionals. The goal for climbing this mountain is to not allow yourself to stay stagnant in your pain. Although there is no timeline or standard grief process, I believe that after a year you should feel a lot of progress and you should be sleeping well and waking up with a bright mind. A good night's sleep is crucial to your mental and physical health, and is a necessary component to a healthy life, whether you are going through a loss or not.

On average, an adult needs around eight hours of sleep. You need this more than ever. Your body and mind needs to rest in order to gain mental clarity, and for your body systems to heal. Make an appropriate amount of sleep a priority in your life and one of your tools for healing.

## Challenge:

Getting good sleep may require some diligence on your part. Refrain from caffeine after about 2 or 3 pm. If you are an all-day coffee or tea drinker, try to find an alternative, or cut out the caffeine all together. It may take some time, but soon your body will adjust. Also, you may have heard that a glass of wine or a cocktail before bed as a nightcap is a good idea. Well, it's an okay idea at 6 p.m., but not 11 p.m. According to a report by the National Institute of Health, alcohol at later hours can interrupt your sleep cycle. Timothy Roehrs and Thomas Roth of the Sleep Disorders and Research Center in Detroit, MI. claim that among non-alcoholics, the occasional use of alcohol as a sleep aid can improve sleep *initially*, but that people tend to develop a tolerance for its effects pretty quickly. At this point, the probability for a healthy sleep pattern diminishes significantly.[9]

Instead, try eating a healthy diet of super foods a few hours before you lie down to sleep. Talk with your health care provider before considering any dietary changes.

Here are some super foods that can help you fall asleep:

**Almonds:** Almonds have a high magnesium content. When a body is low in magnesium, it is harder to fall asleep. Just a handful of raw or dry roasted almonds, or a tablespoon of almond butter an hour before bed can help promote good sleep and muscle relaxation.

**Cherries:** Cherries will help naturally boost your body's own melatonin levels. Try sipping on tart cherry juice a few hours before going to bed.

**Kale:** Loaded with calcium, green leafy vegetables like kale help the brain use tryptophan to manufacture

---

[9] Roehrs, Timothy, and Thomas Roth. "*Sleep, Sleepiness, Sleep Disorders and Alcohol Use and Abuse.*"

melatonin. Mustard greens and spinach are other good options.

**Bananas:** Bananas contain natural muscle relaxants, which helps induce sleep. They also contain magnesium and potassium, which promotes sleep, and B6, which the body needs to make the sleep-inducing hormone melatonin.

**Yogurt:** The calcium in yogurt and other dairy products will help you fall asleep more quickly and avoid the wandering mind that we've all experienced.

**Jasmine Rice:** Jasmine rice, with its high glycemic index is another super food. It boosts the production of tryptophan and serotonin in the blood, which encourage sleep.

**Chamomile Tea:** Drinking a cup of chamomile tea before bed will help you sleep. The tea is associated with an increase of glycine, a chemical that relaxes nerves and muscles and acts like a mild sedative.

There are many other super foods, such as broccoli, grapefruit, strawberries, miso soup, fish, bell peppers, chickpeas, and watermelon, all of which can help aid in your drifting off. You might also consider herbal supplements, which can be very beneficial in helping you achieve healthy sleep.

Sleep is one of your most important healing tools. View it as a positive thing in your life that you are thankful for. Something that is offered to you for free. A way to give your mind a rest, and time for the cells and organs in your body to heal. Go to bed with the thought process of *now I can lay down, put this day to rest, and begin again tomorrow.* Sleep is your transition from one day to the next, so it needs to be nurtured and respected. If you do not get your seven to nine hours, find a way to do so. Talk to a counselor, consult with your doctor, take some supplements, change your diet, get more exercise. Try yoga, meditation, or guided imagery. Stretching before bed has been beneficial for me. Some gentle, restorative stretching or yoga will put your mind at ease and reduce any muscle tension. While stretching, also pay attention to your breath. Long, deep breaths will help you wind down. Also, consider tweaking the little environmental things in your bedroom, such as the amount of light, any noises that are keeping you from sleeping, the TV, cell phone alerts, or the temperature. Typically, a cool, dark, quiet, and calm environment is where we catch the most ZZZZs. Find peace in your sleep.

*Put your thoughts to sleep, do not let them cast a shadow over the moon on your heart. Let go of thinking.*

—RUMI

Misty Nichols

## *Truth #21*

# *Reflect on your dreams*

Immediately after Kris passed away, I started writing in a dream journal. I journaled about every dream I had for a year. To this day, I still write down my dreams when I feel they are significant. The more I analyzed my dreams, the more I realized how truly meaningful they were. Not all of them, but the majority. I could often translate meaning from them that would help me through my healing process. I had recurring dreams about water after Kris passed. Most of the time it was the ocean, sometimes a lake, sometimes a stream, sometimes a pool. I wrote down details about what the water looked like, felt like, how clear it was, how deep it was, if I was in it, and who was with me. Often, if I went to bed stressed out, the water would be dark and murky, or I would jump in the water and not know if I would ever resurface. If I was stressed, I would also fear what was below and around me if I could not see through the water. Most often though, my dreams offered me hope.

In the hopeful dreams, the water was clear and beautiful. I was happy. I was free. The vast ocean signified endless possibilities and beauty. I remember one dream I had in particular while I was at the retreat in California. I was swimming with whales. They were massive, yet peaceful and gentle. They came right up to me and brushed against me as if to say, *Everything is going to be okay, there is divine wisdom guiding you.* I woke up feeling content and connected to my source. I became very thankful for my dreams, and still am.

I also dream of Kris a lot. I had one dream that was very healing for me. It had to do with the guilt I felt for not being there with my family when they found him. I didn't get to say goodbye; I wanted to be there in that moment, the four of us as witnesses, all of us as a family. So one night I had a dream that I was in a field with Kris.

Suddenly he gets shot, and I run over to him. He is heavy in my arms, and his body is warm against me as he slips from consciousness. His chest heaves. I sob, but I am still strong enough to hold him up. I knew I could not save him, but my presence offered comfort. He takes his last breath and I gently lay him down on the ground.

When I awoke, I knew there was a reason for that dream. I didn't wake up sad or depressed. I woke up with a feeling that I had closure, like I was there, like I *did* have a part in that night with my family. That dream told me it was okay. It gave me the feeling of being there, and to me that is truth enough. I believe our loved ones may connect with us in our dreams. I know he would want me to feel contentment and not feel guilt for not being there. I view that dream as a gift, one that offered me some necessary closure and healing.

Sometimes our dreams are analogies. For example, while I was going through my divorce, I had a dream that I was in space, hanging onto something very heavy.

I feel very uncomfortable with this baggage I am holding onto, because I want to explore. I want to be closer to Kris. I want to be free to roam in the vastness and beauty around me. And I wanted to understand it all. Something tells me to let go of what I am holding onto. I look down, and I am holding onto my ex-husband by a rope! This voice tells me that if I let go, I will be able to see Kris and connect with him. Kris is free, and I am not. So I drop the baggage, and this allows me to move on, to have an even clearer memory of my brother, along with a sense of freedom.

That dream really spoke to me. It was clearly an inner guidance or my subconscious trying to help me to let go of the past and all of the hurt that my marriage and divorce brought me. I try to keep this dream in mind anytime I feel I'm holding onto things and people who are no longer doing me any good and are preventing me from moving forward. I had the choice to let go of the negative memories of my ex-husband, and hold on to and cherish the memories of my brother. By taking these mental actions, I was choosing emotional freedom. My visual dream analogy helped me do this.

You should love your dreams, appreciate the humor and fantasy of some of them, the reality of others, and the meaning of many. Learn to embrace your sleep and your dreams.

## *Challenge:*

Keep a dream diary. You could have a completely separate book in which to write your dreams down, or you can just write them within your life journal. Make sure you date your dream entry, and be as specific as possible with the details. Who was there, how did you feel, what were your surroundings? Think about your dream and see if you can make sense of something that can help you in your waking hours. Maybe your dream is suggesting you need to clear some clutter from your life, not be afraid to take a risk, or get closer with a friend or family member. Could be anything. Listen to the subtle or not-so-subtle cues in your dreams. It's like free therapy, and often more precise and accurate. You will find more truth there than you thought, and you will continue to gain understanding as you go back and read your entries later on. Your dreams may represent how you are feeling emotionally and mentally at the time, or they may even forecast a little bit of your life. Our subconscious holds a lot of intuition and wisdom that our conscious mind doesn't. Learn to love, listen to, and respect your dreams.

*Dreams are today's answers to tomorrow's questions.*

—EDGAR CAYCE
Edgar Cayce Readings (C) 1971

# *Truth #22*

# *Keep a connection with your loved one*

Yes, your loved one has left physically, but ask yourself these questions: Can you still see him or her in your mind? Can you still hear him or her in your mind? Can you sometimes just *feel* his or her presence? For me the answer is yes on all accounts. I tend to believe that your loved one is still present with you even after he or she passed on. Just as in Truth #8, which states *God never leaves you*, I believe our loved ones do not leave us either. In whatever capacity you choose, he or she can now be your angel, your comfort, the one whom you call on for wisdom and strength. Listen to your instinct. Does it tell you that he or she is okay and in the presence of peace and love? I would presume so. I believe your loved ones want the same peace and love for you here on earth.

At times I would question my relationship with my brother after he passed. I questioned my own thoughts and feelings. I wondered if I was just making up a positive relationship with him in my mind as some kind of coping mechanism. A way of refusing to let go. After some time though, I surrendered to the spiritual relationship that was forming and held on to it. As I healed, the significance and power of my connection with him made more and more sense. Three months after Kris passed, I viewed him as a source of comfort, knowledge, understanding, and peace. The thought of him and his presence became a form of protection for me, a place of safety and knowledge. So at times I would ask him what he thought of my actions, my thoughts, my feelings, my decisions, and my life. I pondered what I thought he would say, and what he would suggest I do. I listened, and I always knew he was right. His spirit was enveloped in love, forgiveness, and peace. He was near to God. When I was still, I would know the answers. It is very possible to gain understanding from our loved ones. So listen. Listen to what your heart says. Our loved ones speak to our hearts.

Even if you choose not to ask for guidance from your loved one, a relationship can be important. And a relationship may just be the way you connect with that person's memory—the way you remember him or her, the way you think of him or her, and your thoughts of that person. How you *feel* about that person. How you think that person felt or feels about *you*. No matter how you use the relationship in your life, you should come to a place of peace and understanding about your loved one. You should be able to smile when you think of him or her, remembering laughter, humor, and compassion. The good things. Those good things do not need to pass. They are yours to hold on to and cherish. Forever.

## Challenge:

Find your way of connecting to your loved one and hold on to it. Feel it and know it to be true. Feel the presence of the loving relationship. Even if you don't claim a religion, or don't have a deep faith in God or spirituality, you can still count on your own interpretation of your relationship with your loved one, however you choose to do it.

Make your experience your own. Connect with your loved one in a way that can make you smile. Maybe you want to write him or her letters. Write about him or her in your journal. The first few years, I wrote a happy birthday letter to Kris in July. I imagined him sitting next to me. I smiled. I felt him smile. If you want, feel the presence of your loved one, helping you, guiding you, and comforting you in your everyday life or during your tough times. If you feel it, it is real.

It's also important to keep your loved one's spirit alive by talking about him or her with friends and family. Talk about the good times. Reminisce about the moments you shared together and his or her good qualities. Reflect on how he or she helped shape you as a person. And remember, it's okay if you cry. Tears are a sign of love. Just keep your loved one alive in your heart. That is what matters.

*The people we most love do become a physical part of us, ingrained in our synapses, in the pathways where memories are created.*

—MEGHAN O'ROURKE
*The Long Goodbye*

## Truth #23

# *Forgive yourself and others— let go*

Truly forgiving and letting go is extremely important and powerful. You may not even realize how much your memories and attachments are affecting your present life. I came to realize in my mid-30s that our lives are in constant change, which results in an almost constant process of needing to let go. In order to do this, we need to not form attachments to anything. An attachment to something could mean we have a hard time living happily without it. Keep in mind, detachment doesn't have to lead to disconnection. We can have a connection to everything in the universe without becoming mentally or emotionally attached. A strong realization that you can be healthy, happy and whole without the need of something or someone should be the goal. Not that we shouldn't desire a special someone in our lives, or strive for better lives, but the best of things happen to those who are already happy within themselves.

We may let go of some major life events, people, thoughts, and emotions, but more things will always come up that could potentially hold us back. The conscious act of detachment often needs the conscious act of forgiveness. They tend to go hand in hand. Forgiveness leads to freedom. I'm talking about deep and honest forgiveness. Even if you haven't received an apology from someone, you must forgive. Holding on to grudges only hurts you.

I've had to forgive and forgive and forgive. It's practically a daily act. I had to deeply forgive my brother for leaving us, and my husband for the difficult times. I had to forgive myself for things I had said, done, or reacted irrationally to. I couldn't live a healthy life with a constant feeling of anger and resentment toward my ex-husband. Deep down, I believe he was hurting too, and he had his own collection of emotional issues. The guilt he'd suffered was enough, and I wasn't doing any good hanging onto the past. I had to detach. I understood the full perspective of the relationship and how and why it became a downward spiral of negativity. I forgave my ex, knowing that we had both moved on to better lives.

I had to forgive Kris for not allowing me to say a final goodbye and for leaving me behind with difficult questions and seemingly no answers. I had to forgive him for breaking my heart. I had to detach from the sorrow. Some people want to claim that those who take their own lives are selfish. I never once believed that. I never viewed his act as a selfish one. I think it's selfish of me to even consider that. Who am I to ask someone going through hell to continue to live for *me*? Yes, I felt abandoned, but I know he didn't intentionally try to hurt us. He wasn't trying to prove a point or come out a hero. That was not his personality. In fact, he wanted to hide his problems more than anything. I will never understand it all, and I can't put myself exactly where he was mentally on that mid-January day, but he was not acting out of spite or disrespect for his loved ones. Leaving us was his way of surviving. All I need to do is not judge, and forgive. That's what he wants. That's the only way to continue to live and survive in full emotional and mental health. Life is short for all of us. We can assume that those who have passed are rooting us on, hoping we find the love and joy that we deserve. Forgiveness is a necessary step to move in that direction.

We all have events in our pasts that are hurtful or negative. We may feel that someone did us wrong or wronged a loved one. It may be something we did or said to someone, or it may be a reaction we are embarrassed of. It may be an emotion that left an imprint on our heart and mind, or it may be the loss of a person or a job we are struggling to let go of in a healthy manner. These things you let go of may resurface again later in your life, requiring you to let go of them again. The past is simply a collection of memories. It's up to you how you use your memories for your own health, happiness, and benefit.

## *Challenge:*

As you move through your grieving process, you must let go of those memories that do not benefit you any longer. Remember to be like water and forgive your obstacles and surroundings. This doesn't mean you should let go of the memories of someone you have lost. Instead, you should work to evolve them into a different experience for you. For example, instead of allowing the memories of someone you have lost to be ones of sadness, guilt, and pain, learn to remember that person in a positive light. Remember the happy times, remember the moments of joy. Just like in the previous truth, recognize how that person has blessed your life. Allow the memories you have of that person to be positive energy.

Learning not to take anything personally is a habit that can eliminate the effects of being hurt by others, and needing to let go in the first place. Most times, a misunderstanding is to blame for that hurt. Jumping to conclusions and allowing our egos to be bruised easily only causes us unnecessary turmoil. Form the habit in your daily life to not take anything personally. The person who said the hurtful words, your ex, the person who cut you off in traffic, the rude customer service representative, your dad, your mom, your siblings, your boss, your associates, those who have passed on … forgive them all, and don't take their actions personally. Realize that you may not know all the details or the situation that led to their behavior. Rise above it all, and protect your spirit and heart in all circumstances. I'm not suggesting that you be guarded or act as a pushover. You do need to remain open in your personality and protect yourself and others in certain situations, but there are many times in our everyday lives when it is not justified to react or think negatively.

Forgiving yourself is just as important. We all make choices that could be considered wrong, or not ideal. I have a hard time believing in mistakes—when we can learn from absolutely everything we do in our lives—but if we continue to live in a pattern of poor choices, that's when we really need to step back and make some major changes. This would be a matter of revisiting Truth #3, *Be aware of your emotions*. Recognize any negative behavior or patterns that may be creating problems or challenges. As you change your habits and heal, forgive yourself. You may be the only one holding yourself back from forgiveness. If you need to resolve a past situation with someone, do it. Ask them to forgive you and move on. Truly forgive your negative actions, words, or thoughts. Do not hold onto regrets; you deserve freedom from the past. Forgiveness begins and ends with *you*. Love who you are and move on. Recognize your faults, ask for forgiveness, and truly forgive yourself from the center of who you are.

Get out your life journal and write down those people and situations you need to forgive and those memories you need to let go of. I wrote a letter to my brother a couple of months after he passed and told him that I forgave him and that I understood. Actually, I told him that I forgave him the day after he passed, when we viewed him, but again it was a longer process to truly forgive. And it may remain that way forever. Sometimes all it takes is trying to understand the situation from all sides, or just accepting that you do not know the why, and just choosing to let go for the sake of your health and well-being.

*When you forgive yourself, you are forgiven. It is important to understand that forgiveness takes place within your own consciousness. The tense situation is within your own mind; and letting go, releasing it, is within your own power.*

—DAN CUSTER
*The Miracle of Mind Power*

*We must be willing to get rid of the life we've planned, so as to have the life that is waiting for us.*

—JOSEPH CAMPBELL

## *Truth #24*

# *Celebrate your mountaintop*

Recognize when you've reached the top of your mountain, your pinnacle. This is when you are able to say, *I'm happy, I'm healthy, my life is good.* You've let go, you no longer dwell on the past, you love yourself, you feel grounded, you have a renewed purpose, and you look forward to your days ahead. The top of your mountain is not where your grief ends or dissolves or no longer exists. The top of your mountain is where you no longer live *inside* your grief. It no longer consumes you or defines you. It doesn't mask your spirit or the spark in your eye like it once did before. Grief will still live inside you—just in a different way. In the way a loved one remains in your memory and in your heart. The memory is love, and the love is grief. It's all the same at the top of your mountain. As long as your love is unending, so is your grief. Own your beautiful scar.

Your journey does not end there. That mountaintop is not your final destination. Your life will always be in constant change. As other mountains of various grades get placed in front of you, you are able to begin your next journey from the top of the mountain you just climbed. Keep moving forward. There is always more to take in, more to learn, and more to be aware of. The events in your life will continue to change you, yet at the top of each of your mountains, you are wiser, stronger, and more and more able to cope and adapt to any future circumstance.

Always recognize the point where you can look behind you and be proud of what you have accomplished and who you have become or are becoming. It is true that we will never be 100 percent all of the time! We will always experience plateaus and valleys, but what's important is how we grow through the journey. And the traveling gets easier as we use what we have learned from the past as tools—our soul gear. Feel grateful for the climb. Recognize your accomplishments, and don't forget to mark this significant milestone.

## *Challenge:*

Do something for yourself to congratulate you. You could simply go to the woods on a pretty day and just be thankful and make it special in your own way. Go some place that is inspiring to you or a place you love and cherish. Maybe it's a loved one's gravesite. Maybe it's the water. Maybe it's your own back yard. Maybe it's a wheat field. Maybe it's a city you've always wanted to visit. Maybe it's a trip to the beach or the mountains. Maybe it's a different country. Maybe you choose to take someone with you who recognizes and appreciates your accomplishments. Maybe you choose to go alone. This moment is for you. You have earned it, and you deserve to be where you are at. You deserve this happiness. Take your life journal and write about it. This is an important day you won't want to forget. Make it your moment of achievement, knowing that you put forth the hard work and it will continue to pay off, forever. What a climb. Congratulations.

*Blessed is the one who finds wisdom, and the one who gets understanding, for the gain from her is better than gain from silver and her profit better than gold. She is more precious than jewels, and nothing you desire can compare to her.*

Proverbs 3:13-15

*Every day you may make progress. Every step may be fruitful. Yet there will stretch out before you an ever-lengthening, ever-ascending, ever-improving path. You know you will never get to the end of the journey. But this, so far from discouraging, only adds to the joy and glory of the climb.*

—SIR WINSTON CHURCHILL

# Acknowledgements

My deepest gratitude extends to many people—people who have been close to me for years and others who have been just glimpses on my path. I have been touched by the hearts, hands, and words of some of the most loving and tender-hearted individuals. Oftentimes I have not felt worthy of such unselfish gestures and loving words, but I have learned that we each have a time to give unto others, and we each have a time to receive. I would not be where or who I am today without these people in my life. They are as much a part of this book as I am. I hope to give back to these people and many others for the rest of my living days. First and foremost, my family:

Thank you, Kris—my brother, my friend, and my inspiration for this book. As hard as it was to accept your short earthly life, I am at peace. Just as I know you are. Our times spent together will forever be some of my fondest memories. You always told me that one day you wanted to help others who needed help. Others who were down, those who felt lonely, lost and sad. Those who struggled finding their places in this world. Although you aren't here to speak face to face with these people, I am here to help relay your message of hope and understanding. I hope to do your mission justice. I hope you understand my reasoning for exposing your hardships. I trust that you believe that through this honesty, incredible healing and growth is the return. Kris, thank you for your friendship. It is real. Thank you for your kind and humble heart. It is inspiring. Your ability to love and respect people at all times is a true testament of your spirit. You told me love is the answer. Yes, love is always the answer.

Thank you, Mom, for being the true example of grace and unconditional love and my strength and security in times of uncertainty. Thank you for being an example of non-judgment, humility, and patience. Your kind spirit is infectious and will always be an inspiration. Thank you for supporting me through this journey and loving me the way a mother should.

Thank you, Dad, I know I can always count on you regardless of the situation. I always know that if times get tough, you are always ready to help hold me up. Thank you for being the intuitive and insightful man you are. Thank you for being our family's rock. Thank you for loving me the way a father should.

Thank you to my sister, who's been a constant in my life—a friend who has held my burdens as if they were her own. Thank you for crying with me, laughing with me, and listening to me, as if we share the same heart. Your unselfish spirit is undeniable. Thank you for being my closest friend in times of hardship and also during the best of times.

Thank you to my brother-in law, who gave advice and support to me as if we were blood. Thank you for your patience in times of turmoil and hardship. You are a strong and understanding man. Thank you for taking me in as a sister and caring so much for my family in times of need.

My sincerest gratitude also goes to my friend Charles. A true testament of patience, generosity, understanding, empathy and love. A humble spirit who has been a mentor of mine for many years. Thank you Charles for listening and not judging. Thank you for reading this book in its rawest form with misspellings and grammatical errors. Your mother is oh so proud of you for your huge heart and accomplishments.

Thank you to my dear girlfriends: Mo, Jenny, Lara, Christin, Abi, Jill, Lisa, and Lauren. You all are strong and amazing women who have each played a significant role in my life. Thank you to Mary and Mia—and the inspiring people who supported me in Laguna Beach. Thank you to the friends and co-workers I met in St John; you all have the freest spirits, and it's intoxicating. Thank you, Yvonne, and my work family at the spa; you gave me a safe and positive place to work while I was getting on my feet again, and after. Thank you to my editors, Jen and Susannah, and my graphic designer, Kevin. Your patience is a virtue!

Lastly, thank you for taking time to read this book, and also to those who have reached out to me to express *their* losses; I appreciate your brave open hearts and honest stories.

You all have allowed me to feel comfortable enough to break down my walls and be vulnerable and honest. You've stood by my side while I was broken, and also when I was whole again. Thank you for allowing me to be me, all the while finding a *better* me.

# Bibliography

Beattie, Melody. *Finding Your Way Home: A Soul Survival Kit.* San Francisco: HarperSanFrancisco, 1998.

O'Rourke, Meghan. *The Long Goodbye.* New York: Riverhead, 2011.

Maraboli, Steve. *Unapologetically You: Reflections on Life and the Human Experience.* Port Washington, NY: Better Today, 2013.

Strayed, Cheryl. *Tiny Beautiful Things: Advice on Love and Life from Dear Sugar.* New York: Vintage, 2012.

Tolle, Eckhart. *The Power of Now: A Guide to Spiritual Enlightenment.* Novato, CA: New World Library, 1999.

"Fact Sheet on Stress." NIMH RSS. Web. 15 Feb. 2016. http://www.nimh.nih.gov/health/publications/stress/index.shtml

Fox, Kenneth R. *"The Influence of Physical Activity on Mental Well-being."* Public Health Nutrition PHN 2.3a (1999).

Roehrs, Timothy, and Thomas Roth. *"Sleep, Sleepiness, Sleep Disorders and Alcohol Use and Abuse."* Sleep Medicine Reviews 5.4 (2001): 287-97.

Made in the USA
Charleston, SC
26 June 2016